The Amoral Elephant

The Rational Herdsman

The Amoral Elephant

Globalization and the Struggle for Social Justice in the Twenty-First Century

William K. Tabb

Monthly Review Press
New York

Library of Congress Cataloging-in-Publication Data

Tabb, William K.
   The amoral elephant: globalization and the struggle for social justice in the
   twenty-first century / William K. Tabb.
      p.cm
   Includes bibliographical references and index.
   ISBN 1-58367-036-X (alk. paper) — ISBN 1-58367-037-8 (alk. paper)
   1. International economic relations—Moral and ethical aspects.
   2. Globalization—Moral and ethical aspects. 3. Capitalism—Moral
      and ethical aspects. 4. Social justice. I. Title.

   HF1359.T332 2001
   337—dc21   2001016410

ISBN 1-58367-036-X (paper)
ISBN 1-58367-037-8 (cloth)

Monthly Review Press
122 West 27th Street
New York, NY 10001

Manufactured in Canada
10 9 8 7 6 5 4 3 2

Contents

CHAPTER ONE

Globalization and the Politics of the Twenty-First Century

"Seattle Shock"

Turning points in historical consciousness are hard to call as they are occurring. Yet for the tens of thousands of people from around the world who converged in Seattle in November of 1999 to protest World Trade Organization (WTO) policies and, more broadly, corporate globalization, and for the millions more around the world who supported the concerns of the demonstrators, something very significant had happened. In the waning moments of the twentieth century, an alternative future for the post–Cold War world system could be glimpsed. The protest brought together environmentalists, trade unionists, Third World subsistence farmers and their supporters, advocates for debt forgiveness and others. They successfully shut down the opening session of the WTO meeting and contributed significantly to the failure of what President Clinton and others had hoped would be a new round of trade and investment liberalization.

The "street heat" may also have inspired the delegates inside the meetings who resisted the imposition of the U.S. agenda. The "battle in Seattle" thus became a prism—clouded to be sure by the tear gas and the pepper spray as well as the cacophony of views represented and the competing messages projected—through which theories of how the global political economy works and can work are being discussed and debated in the early twenty-first century. These begin by making manifest the discontent over the negative impacts not only of globalization but of the neoliberal policies of the global state economic governance institutions—the World Trade Organization, the International Monetary Fund (IMF), and the World Bank (WB).

Mainstream media commentators have reacted with indignation at such unruly disruption of what was to them so obviously a good thing, free trade. The Seattle protests have been presented by establishment voices not as a part of that debate but as disruption of it. The "Seattle Shock," as *Business Week* called it in an editorial warning of a popular backlash against "our very economic system," reflected growing awareness that issues once confined to quiet conference rooms in which trade experts and treasury secretaries met were now burning issues for millions of people. In the *New York Times*, columnist Thomas Friedman raged at anti-WTO protesters as "flat-earth advocates" duped by knaves like Pat Buchanan. "What's crazy," he complained, "is that the protesters want the WTO to become precisely what they accuse it of already being—a global government. They want it to set more rules—their rules, which would impose our labor and environmental standards on everyone else." [1]

The *Economist* ran a cover story in response to the Seattle protests, depicting the plight of a young South Asian girl and stating that "without trade" she was unlikely to get education or health care. "Forbidding her to work won't help her," the *Economist* declared; "Trade is about greater opportunity for millions rather than privileges for the few." [2] Martin Wolf wrote in the *Financial Times*: "What the protestors against globalism share is dislike of the market economy. This passion brought the cranks, bullies and hypocrites to Seattle." [3] After the subsequent protest against the WB and IMF in April 2000, he continued in this vein: "This week, in Washington, D.C., thousands of prosperous people will demonstrate in favor of the perpetuation of mass poverty." [4]

What these responses have in common is their claim that any effort to promote different rules on how trade should occur and to redefine the terms on which globalization was taking place was really an effort to return to the past. Friedman associates the protests with the xenophobia of Buchanan and its racist overtones. The commentators assume that there are no choices other than those that they favor. Rather than simply disagreeing with the politics of anti-WTO protest, these commentators deny that any coherent political perspective can inform such protest at all. They presume to see the process of managing globalization as purely technical, and profess to find unintelligible the protesters' often-stated commitment to democratizing a process of deciding the global rules rather than leaving them to the discretion of secretive elites.

The scale of the Seattle protest was in part the result of such underhanded methods being exposed. For years, government representatives had been negotiating a proposed Multilateral Agreement on Investment intended to speed up and lock in the process of opening markets, removing obstacles to faster globalization. This negotiation was curtailed when a Canadian non-governmental organization (NGO) posted a leaked copy of the working document on a web site and a worldwide protest movement sprung into being, effectively stopping the agreement. The success of this campaign—and other grassroots protests against corporate policy demands—emboldened the protesters in Seattle and later protesters in the streets of Washington and Prague and wherever else the new decision makers of the global economy have met.

The media pundits who dismissed the protests could not explain why a process intended to assist the poor needed to be controlled by the rich. In Seattle, the elite and their invited guests met in private boardrooms while everyone else waited outside to hear what the powerful had decided for them. Many people learned for the first time at Seattle of the existence of the QUAD, the Quadrilateral Group of Trade Ministers, which was formed in 1981 and acts as the informal committee guiding the global trade regime. Before public meetings of the WTO, members of the QUAD—the United States, the European Union, Japan, and Canada—meet privately, making key decisions without the participation of other representatives of the world community. Once the QUAD reaches agreement, a larger, select group of twenty to thirty countries are invited to come together in informal meetings. Only after that do the 143 members of the WTO discuss and vote on proposals that are typically, by this point, faits accomplis. The poor countries of the periphery are forced to fall in line by the pressure of the economic and political muscle arrayed against them.

Officials that represent the QUAD are closely linked to the corporations they serve. Personnel move back and forth between lobbyists for and leadership of giant corporations, banks, legal firms, and what is called the public service sector. The Business Roundtable in the United States, the European Roundtable of Industrialists, Canada's Business Council on National Issues, and Japan's Keidanren have an enormous influence on the decisions that are made by the QUAD. The QUAD policy-making advisory committees are headed by important CEOs. They consult closely with the officials who attend the QUAD meetings as well as the more general gatherings. Through this transmission belt, the desires of the dominant factions of the capitalist class are first negotiated and then imposed on weaker capitals and on the workers of the world. For some time, the use of this procedure had been accepted as inevitable. In Seattle, Third World delegates, perhaps emboldened by the presence of the demonstrators, publicly criticized it.

There was very little media attention when World Bank premises in New Delhi were occupied in protest against the destruction of livelihood and the environment by the WTO and the World Bank. Hundreds of Adivasis, indigenous peoples from the Indian state of Madya Pradesh, blocked the World Bank building, covering it with posters, graffiti, cow dung and mud, and singing traditional songs and chanting slogans.[5] The *Economist* had argued that the young Indian woman in its cover picture and others of the world's poor needed the policies that have been forced on developing countries by the global financial institutions. But it gave no publicity to the New Delhi protest. Nor did the *Economist* cover the tour of the Indian environmental activist Vandana Shiva, who was touring the United States at the same time as the New Delhi protests. She told an audience somewhat different than the one typically addressed by the financial press that

> All across India's 7,000 km coastline, and this is what I was working on just before I left, World Bank financing has created a cancerous growth of industrial farms creating a saline desert, devastating coastal ecosystems and coastal people who have been protesting about these policies. We reached the Supreme Court. The Indian Supreme Court ruled that this activity was destructive and must be stopped. And then the World Bank and its national credit agencies applied pressure on the government to try and undo the laws.[6]

Shiva cited an earlier incident in 1984, when the World Bank would only provide loans for deepening wells in a time of drought if there was agreement to adopt sugarcane as a cash crop. According to Shiva, this created a water famine within five years and forced the country into deeper debt. As activists from around the world come to America and gain a hearing, the cost of economic governance institution strategies become more widely discussed and pressure builds for them to open the process of policy formation and review.

Trade unionists from around the world have also come to the United States with stories of exploitation and violence they have had to endure at the hands of U.S. transnational corporations and their suppliers. The sympathy from American workers for such repression and the condemnation of the denial of labor rights comes in some measure from fear that if such conditions can be imposed on workers over there, then conditions here can be pushed down as well.

After denouncing the selfishness of protesters, many commentaries and editorial opinions ended up acknowledging the justice of the demonstrators' concerns. A number of accounts start by denouncing "thuggery," "special interest groups," the "ragamuffins" and "demagogues" and yet end up in effect supporting the logic of "the more rational protesters" and their arguments.[7] The press denounced the AFL-CIO as protectionist and selfish, yet when *Business Week* discussed the global backlash it noted that

> Despite a 3 percent unemployment rate for American adults, hundreds of thousands of people are still being fired every year. As companies restructure and adapt to the New Economy, they are churning their workforces. Many operations are being sent overseas. In the '80s, only blue-collar workers faced this problem. In the '00s, white-collar employees are watching their jobs migrate to India and Ireland.[8]

When it turned to the policies of the global state economic governance institutions, *Business Week* agreed with the demonstrators: "Long-held IMF prescriptions for solving international financial crises are losing support. Bailing out private banks while depressing growth and forcing unemployment higher—a strategy the IMF initially pursued in Asia—is no longer acceptable. . . . Nor is the World Bank's traditional focus on promoting Third World development by financing huge steel mills and enormous dams."[9] And as for corporate responsibility, or irresponsibility, and use of sweated labor, again the *Business Week* editorial writers seemed to endorse the demonstrators' critique: "Corporations, for their part, should begin to take direct responsibility for the working conditions in their operations overseas. . . . Relying on middlemen to supply goods and turning a blind eye to the way they are produced is no longer acceptable." [10] They are particularly aware of campus protests that have highlighted the use of prison and child labor and horrible working conditions for women. Such practices "taint" free trade and so multinationals should act responsibly.

Although these commentators had not thought to raise such criticisms themselves, they are now forced to acknowledge their validity. So if the pundits are willing to concede so much of the legitimacy of the protesters' cause, why are they so hostile to their protests? Part of the reason is that through these protests the larger picture of the way the political economy operates is becoming clearer to larger numbers of people thought to be relatively apolitical, encouraging them to become politically involved. The movement for global social justice presents an interpretation to them of their own material conditions and the larger social relations of actually existing capitalism suggesting they may be understood through the protesters' understanding of the operation of our global politico-economic system. The corporate strategy has been to acknowledge that people feel a great deal of discomfort and uncertainty and that they are fearful of the impacts of globalization. In a Pew Research Center nationwide survey of April 1999, while 43 percent of respondents said that in the future a global economy would help average Americans, 52 percent said that it would hurt them. Corporate public relations efforts distinguish between such "understandable emotional responses" and what they represent as the reality: these changes are good for us, even if change is always unsettling. Keeping to this general line allows them to strenuously avoid questions about the cost specifics and the exact benefits of globalization. It is easy to see why.

At the same time, NGOs and popular mass movements have become increasingly significant players in the struggle to redefine economic and political rules appropriate to our era of globalization. Tension between these organizations of civil society and the instrumentalities of the dominant trilateral governments in North America, Europe, and Japan over the rules governing trade, investment, and finance have spilled into the streets. Direct action, civil disobedience and other tactics by those who feel unrepresented in the closed meetings of the emergent international state governing councils have started a conversation that has involved a widening audience. People exercising their rights of free speech and assembly have broken through the elite monologue proclaiming "our model of globalization is inevitable, our model is the only model and there is no alternative, our model is good for you."

At the heart of all of these developments and controversies is the question of the definition of globalization—a capacious category that encompasses many aspects and meanings. The term depicts a process of interconnectedness among states and societies. It describes how events and activities in one part of the world come to have significant consequences for distant people and communities. A reduction in the cost and an increase in the speed of communication and transportation deepen this process. It is not simply about economics or even growing cultural and social interdependencies of the global village that drinks Coke and watches Disney.

Globalization remakes the world's trade and finance regimes, and also redefines awareness at a most local and intimate level, affecting how people see themselves, the life space of their children, their ethnicity. Multiple identities change as a result of the forces of globalization.

Globalization is understood by most people as a problem of markets expanding beyond people's capacity to affect them. Given profit-maximizing behavior on the part of capitalists—who do not take into account the environmental costs of their activity, impacts on communities, or the need to pay for basic public goods, and who treat working people as commodities—globalization may be irreversible. But the form it takes is not inevitable and the manner in which capitalist accumulation is now taking place on a world scale is unsustainable. Globalization, in short, is about relations of relative power, dependence as much as exchange, and how otherness becomes naturalized or provokes resistance. Far from being a merely technical matter, globalization is a deeply political process. The struggle to define its meaning will structure much of the politics of the twenty-first century.

The Amoral Elephant

In his novel *Catch-22* Joseph Heller created one of the memorable characters of modern literature. Milo Minderbinder sells the parachutes of pilots flying into battle for their silk value. He is frightening in his amorality and funny in that painful way that makes you laugh not "'till it hurts" (although sometimes that too), but in response to the black humor that is so painful. In a 1998 interview, Heller speaks of looking around and seeing his archetypal creation, the indefatigable unprincipled entrepreneur, everywhere. "Like capitalism, he was amoral, he provided good things and bad things. He didn't think about consequences. He was anti-social and unpatriotic. In fact, he was a forerunner of the multinational corporation and the global economy." [11] The world today experiences this sort of competitive war as the rules we have grown accustomed to are undermined by a global neoliberalism, which supposedly creates freedom. But it is an amoral freedom at best, benefiting transnational corporations and international finance.

George Soros, the billionaire hedge fund operator and social change philanthropist, is not alone in seeing such "freedom" as producing disastrous outcomes for economies around the world and creating the threat of global collapse. Soros shares Heller's belief that amoral greed drives the world, but fears its consequences. He remarks, "I believe markets are amoral. The problem is that they are not always stable. They frequently swing to excesses. That's why I say that markets, instead of swinging like a pendulum, can sometimes be a wrecking ball. . . ." [12]

As a businessman, Soros has competed with great personal success in these markets. When he does so, he says, he functions as an amoral man. He competes as an amoral man, he says, because "if I allowed moral considerations to influence my investment decisions, it would render me an unsuccessful competitor. And it would not in any way influence the outcome because there would be someone else to take my place at only a marginally different price." [13] As a responsible member of society, George Soros may be concerned with moral issues but he would not be a successful capitalist long if he allowed such considerations to direct his business practice. He says there must be rules to control what capitalists are allowed to do and how they are allowed to do it. For without such rules the very stability of society is put in danger.

Impersonal markets can wreak havoc as their wild swings, the rapid flow of capital into and out of countries, the sudden drop in market values for corporate shares, real estate or currencies, bring to a sudden end our assumed realities. The impact of the wrecking ball is to suddenly take away the order that ordinary people depend upon, not as speculators but rather as prisoners of these larger structuring forces. The pendulum swings and they find their livelihoods gone, their lives disrupted perhaps beyond repair. It is the anxiety of such forebodings that sits so uncomfortably with the techno-optimism of skyrocketing stock markets and the technological wonders of the new information economy.

The intensity of societal concern about these matters, and even the ways in which such questions are asked, change with time and the state of the economy. In periods of deep structural transformation the destabilizing force of change raises disturbing questions that flow from people's daily experience as workers and citizens. They try to make sense of the elephant. The elephant is capitalism—so large a presence in our lives that we are like the blind men (with their elephant) who each grasp some seeming local truth. One puts his arms around a leg and announces confidently that it is a tree trunk. Another leans against the great body and says "the wall of this old fortress is strong and thick." Another grasps the tail and triumphantly proclaims it a rope. Still another, feeling an ear, recognizes the giant leaf of a jungle plant. Each is confident that he understands the totality from the local experiential information he has obtained. And of course those who ride atop the elephant have a different experience of its nature than those who are trod beneath its feet. The elephant itself is amoral.

Globalization is perhaps the ultimate Rorschach test of *fin-de-siècle* politics. It remains the amorphous form our elephant takes at the start of the new millennium. Our vision of it remains imperfect. Our task is made more difficult because our great elephant seems constantly to change its shape, even as the basic elements of its nature remain, or remain constant through these dramatic transformations. To others it is continually becoming a new creature and not the same animal at all. The central discourse of the early twenty-first century is making sense of the same old elephant, now seen in a new and different guise.

Debating the Ethics of Globalization

The field of debate on globalization is large, complex, and rapidly changing. But it is possible to distinguish a number of levels on which questions concerning globalization are posed. Although these are always interrelated, the most conspicuous of them is debate on the moral question.

On the question of whether globalization is "good" or "bad," opinion is divided along predictable lines. Those who benefit from it, or think they benefit from it, or will come to benefit from it, like it and don't want interference. Those who lose out think that they will lose out, or fear, the disruption and social cost of globalization demand that if changes are "good" overall than efforts should be made to distribute the benefits more fairly so that some do not pay too high a price while others benefit disproportionately. Since the losers become poorer (and are often among the poor to start with) and the winners, already among the most well off, become richer, there is some justice in these demands. Some who may benefit in the short term are indeed among the most marginalized of those who have become part of the "modern" economy through the globalization process. Of course, in the process they are exploited by the powerful, but the powerful and their intellectual allies say it is better to be exploited than ignored.

But gratitude for being exploited quickly fades as workers see who gets the lion's share of the fruits of their labor. Then we hear the classic refrain of the masters, "they are so ungrateful for everything we have done for them." The debate is intense and often angry. The oppressed confront more than intellectual arguments. They face the repressive apparatus of the state and the constraining manipulation of international agencies of power, the IMF, the WTO and the rest. Power concedes as little as it can.

What may be called the liberal view of globalization (liberal in the nineteenth-century usage; the sort of liberalism embraced in the twentieth century by Bill Clinton and Tony Blair) supposes that exchange is a voluntary and mutually beneficial process, a positive-sum game. The presumption in this segment of the globalization literature is that there will be harmony and pretty much everyone will (eventually) benefit. The differing regulatory rules of individual nation-states that seek to

protect older modes, now less efficient for the reorganization of production in the light of new developments in technological possibilities,
can be seen as market imperfections that are best swept aside as globalization proceeds.

But this is already to assume a very specific basis for judgment, which
equates moral worth with productive efficiency. It is to take the cultural
norms produced by the contemporary process of globalization as the
standard by which to judge it. The revolutionary capacity of capitalism
to develop the forces of production should not be a surprise. Its cultural
impact is more controversial. For some critics the problem is not so
much the exploitation of Third World workers or the damage to the
environment but that, as one sign seen at the IMF–WB protest said,
"Capitalism stultifies." It is the "five hundred channels and nothing on,"
on which this critique centers. That Americans spend an average of four
hours a day in front of a television set represents to some an "escape
from freedom," in which the inauthenticity of the system is what is most
damaging as everything is reduced to a product and the assault of
advertising diminishes human potential to that of making a buck.

Debating the Economics of Globalization

Discussion of the moral implications of globalization comes to turn,
then, on how growth is understood. It could be argued that this reflects
a narrow view of the moral issues at stake. But the argument should still
be assessed in its own terms. The case for a positive interpretation of
globalization assumes the triumph of a new economy that is fundamentally restructuring the world for the better. This is the second level of
debate on globalization.

The first piece of evidence usually cited (at this writing) in support
of the thesis that globalization is an economic success is the performance
of the American stock market. The wider Washington consensus model
must be the right one—look at how rich those who follow it become.
In this optimistic interpretation the stock market is considered to reflect
the performance of the real economy in some fairly straightforward and
unproblematic manner. Thus *Business Week* began a cover story on "The
Triumph of the New Economy" by observing an astonishing increase in

the stock market's valuation of the American economy. Asking rhetorically whether the market was crazy, it answered "hardly." The global market and the information revolution had created a fundamentally new situation. A supporting argument declared that inflation was dead because of global competition. Domestic producers have to confront competition from low-cost imports and so must constantly cut costs. Deregulation is another factor in the reduction of costs. The Telecommunications Act of 1986 led to dramatic reduction in the cost of information transfer over distance. The Internet, digital wireless, low-orbit satellites, and broadband networks undercut monopoly power and force further deregulation everywhere, allowing global networks to emerge and encouraging easier and less costly reorganization of the global economy. New technologies associated with computerization fundamentally enable the new economy to penetrate all aspects of the society with important productivity enhancing impacts.

However, greater control over information is also greater control over people. That wealth is generated is true. The question of whether these changes are an unalloyed blessing for workers and consumers is more problematic.

That globalization is tied to economic innovation of unprecedented profitability developed in the core—financial services, telecommunications, business services such as consulting and accounting, consumer services such as fast food and Internet retailing—often gets lost in the awareness of the dislocations, job loss, and deep recession in so much of the world. Like the enclosures at the dawn of capitalist development, transformations involve regressive redistribution as the leading edge of capitalist development sweeps the old ways aside, ignoring the social costs of its restructuring. From the point of view of the leading segments of the capitalist class this is always the way it must be—but of course they profit from the pain their activities generate. They also gain at the expense of capitalists who have fallen behind. Throughout Asia, to take a current example, depositors in the once miracle economies have lined up to get their money out of local banks and put them in Citibank and branches of other Western financial giants. Firms, that not much earlier had been contenders in global markets, are forced to sell once profitable divisions and their entire companies to foreign investors as a result of bankruptcy.

Local control ebbs. Inequality grows. The increasing contradiction between wealth and poverty produces oppositional responses and demand for social control of capital, the reaction to the distributional growth that creates great wealth for the few even as it advances the forces of production, punishing many whose lives are disrupted and whose often tenuous security is destroyed. The cost of unfettered growth produces the social movement for its control. Capitalism is a system of redistributional growth. The dynamic of social change derives from its very nature. Capitalism's development is thus a more complex process then either its celebrants or denouncers acknowledge.

The super-bullish view of the twenty-first century's unlimited possibilities is epitomized by yet another *Business Week* cover story. An essay entitled "You Ain't Seen Nothing Yet" suggests that impressive growth will continue because "the innovation pipeline is fuller than it has been in decades." [14] Its writers suggest that we are only at the start of a powerful surge in technology. They contemplate the building of new materials atom by atom and customized cures for cancer by drugmakers who would have "the bar code" for each of our individual DNAs. Based on such promises for nanotechnologies and biotechnologies one can see why efficient capital market theorists believe the stock market is right to evaluate the future prospects of the U.S. economy and its leading new growth sectors in such extravagant terms.

In a similar, if less rapturous tone Alan Greenspan, chair of the Federal Reserve System, in his semi-annual Humphrey-Hawkins testimony before Congress in February 1999, said: "It seems likely that the synergies of advances in laser, fiber-optic, satellite and computer technologies with older technologies have enlarged the pool of opportunities to achieve a rate of return above the cost of capital." But if Mr. Greenspan appears to be a convert to new economy-think he had for some time worried about whether a speculative bubble was occurring. In late 1996 Greenspan famously warned of its "irrational exuberance." He said in this testimony that "Whether or not it's gripped by irrational exuberance is an issue that you won't really know for sure except after the fact." The market valuations on Wall Street markets were however high enough to give him "concerns." Warren Buffett, one of the most admired and copied investors of our age, interviewed as the Dow passed the 10,000 mark, offered the view that the stock market had become "overheated." [15] Others, from then Secretary of the Treasury Robert Rubin to George Soros, expressed similar misgivings. But the market kept heading north, with new technology stocks leading the way. This expansion long outlasted the previous record length of a market run-up, the six-year spree that ended in the 1929 crash. The *fin-de-siècle* boom in American equity markets literally had no parallel in market history.

From the beginning of the 1980s, companies such as Microsoft, Cisco Systems, Intel, and Lucent (all among the top seven U.S. companies by market value) saw their valuations rise exponentially compared to the old line slow- growth and no-growth industrials. In the 1920s companies like RCA and General Motors, which then represented the new industrial makeup of the economy, were a force in the run-up of the Dow between 1925 and 1929—before the market crashed and share prices fell 89 percent from their peak to the low of 1932. The talk of a new economy and permanent prosperity has been heard before. At the turn of the millennium the leading "new economy" corporations were information oriented, a new elite of knowledge-based capital firms. Once new ideas are embodied in corporate form, the first to become well established and achieve scale in manufacturing, marketing, or product development see increasing returns and dominate their industries. The best performers at the turn of the century, those whose stock prices were rising by well over a thousand percent a year, had names like Digital Lightwave, Broadvision, VeriSign, DoubleClick, and Qual-Comm. A third of the year's top fifty performers hadn't been traded three years earlier but were worth many billions of dollars now.

Those opposing a benign view of globalization stress not only the potential instability of what looked to them like a bubble economy in which the high stock values could not be sustained, but pointed to the costs of the transition to the new economy and their incidence. Those who are hurt are a very different group than those who receive the greatest benefits of the process. Capitalist growth is not only crisis prone, but by its nature biased toward increasing the power of capital over people as consumers, citizens, and workers. Through its sales effort it pushes commodification of social life. Satisfaction comes from individual ownership of things, new possessions felt to be essential for status reasons, as a source of self-respect. The unequal distribution of wealth not only intensifies envy, but provides the material basis for political influence, the capacity to shape public discourse and state decisions. The choice of technologies is not innocent of the desire to more effectively control labor, promote the sales effort, and accumulation.

At the same time, in recent years American companies are moving both up market and down market as growing inequality is changing America from a middle-class nation to a country of rich and poor. Consider that in 1987 American airlines received 9.5 percent of their domestic revenues from first- and business-class seats. In 1997 it was 22 percent. Stock market wealth is part of the story, but the bottom 80 percent of households own less than 2 percent of the total value of equity holdings (including pension funds, IRAs, mutual funds, and Keoghs).[16] It is not surprising, or at least it shouldn't be, that the richest 10 percent of American families received 85 percent of the three trillion-plus dollar increase in stock market valuation between 1989 and 1997.

Since 1980 the wealthiest fifth of the population has had a 21 percent growth of its income while those in the bottom 60 percent have seen their living standard stagnate or fall. The figures can be sliced and diced in many ways, and are quite dramatic. Between 1980 and 1995 the inflation adjusted earnings of the top 10 percent of adult full-time earners rose by 11 percent while the median adult worker's wage fell by 4 percent and the wages of the bottom tenth of the distribution fell by 10 percent.[17] The highest earning fifth buy most of the new cars sold and from retailers to hotels to banks the best customers are targeted for special benefits since they are where the big profits come from. *Business Week,* featuring a cover story on "Executive Pay: It's Out of Control," explains that the bull market is making managers with stock options very rich and the bull market is "feeding unconscionable growing inequality." [18]

Economic anxiety kept company with the bull market as the social contract between employer and employee broke down and massive layoffs at profitable firms became the norm.[19] A sense of job insecurity is quite rational as is the frequently heard comment that "the company is not a very good one to work for but a great one to own stock in."

Studies of job loss in the mid-1990s showed three-quarters of all American households have seen a family member, other relative, friend or neighbor lose a job since 1980. Many laid-off workers return to their old jobs as temps. A Department of Labor survey showed 17 percent of a representative sample of so-called contingent workers (those working part-time or as contract rental workers) had had a previous and different relation to the company that now rents them from a temp agency.[20] More people are being laid off during the expansion of the 1990s than in previous recessions and when they find new jobs they are at substantially lower wages. These trends developed in the longest peacetime expansion in the country's history and go far toward explaining the fear of globalization.

The new technology sectors had been stressed as contributing so importantly to the record market spurt of the 1990s. But in all but the leading high-tech sectors, and in some of them as well, overcapacity became a serious problem by the late 1990s. The *Economist*'s measure of the output gap, the discrepancy between actual output and potential output, on a global scale at the end of the 1990s was its biggest since the Great Depression of the 1930s. With deflation, due to overcapacity and intensified competition, the real burden of debt increased. Total debt in the United States at the end of the 1990s was equal to about 130 percent of GDP. In 1929 it was only 100 percent of GDP. At the end of the 1990s it was 200 percent in Japan where companies were unable to repay debts and most large banks were, by U.S. standards, bankrupt.[21]

By the early twenty-first century, production almost everywhere and in almost all industries was running ahead of consumption and the world appeared headed for a deflationary era (even as stock markets continued into record high territories, thanks to "new economy" expectations). We need to remember that in the Great Depression it was the falling prices (10 percent a year between 1929 and 1933) that increased debt burdens in real terms—deepening and prolonging the crisis. If deflation spreads and deepens the world will be in serious trouble and will risk a cumulative downward cycle as overcapacity leads to fewer sales and more layoffs. Most of the world by the end of the 1990s was in price recession, with producers unable to raise prices because of foreign competition, excess capacity in their industries, and lack of demand for their products. Many parts of the world from Latin America to East Asia had, in the preceding two decades, gone through financial crises in which debt over-extension, financing growth with borrowed monies that could not be repaid when the ability to export slackened, and speculative excess overreached plausible limits.

There are really two debates on the economics of globalization. The first is over whether markets need rules or whether "free" markets and "free" competition (with only the minimalist state protecting property and the sanctity of contracts) are enough. The second is the extent to which capital should be under social regulation, not simply to protect it from itself, but so that the rest of us can place capital under social control to ensure that other social goals are achieved. The first debate is over regulation, of capital in the interest of system stability. The second concerns the desirability, extent, and the content of socialization of capital and the political process through which society makes decisions concerning what to produce, how to produce it, and the ends to which the productive capacity of the political economy will be put. In both contexts, debate on the economics of globalization comes to rest, at this point, on estimates of its historical significance.

The "New Economy": Debating the Historical Meaning of Globalization

There is a widespread view that globalization has introduced a fundamentally new epoch in human history, unlike any that has gone before; that changes taking place in the economy make previous modes of historical analysis redundant. The "information economy," or the "new economy," is the name given to capture the use of the fax machine, the Internet, cellular phones, personal computers, and the digitalization of information that allows faster storage and data retrieval of information concerning consumers and the flow of products. Between the early 1980s and the late 1990s business spending in the United States on information equipment as a share of GDP came close to tripling.

Information technology pioneered in this country is transforming economies everywhere. As marketing spreads throughout the world, consolidations, mergers, and acquisitions proceed apace and the dramatic centralization and concentration of capital on a world scale bring profits to transnationals. By the mid-1990s, when investment in computers and software accounted for three-quarters of the increase in all business investment, information technology was recognized as the engine of growth in this country even if its impacts were hard to measure statistically. Popular access through the World Wide Web makes comparison shopping easier, intensifies competition to the advantage of buyers while delivering larger potential markets to sellers, and helps smaller companies whose specialized products can get exposure and be delivered over great distance through time-conscious package services.

When discussing a particular period of historical development, some people prefer to stress continuity, others transformation. Surely there are dramatically new, even revolutionary aspects to the contemporary economy, but then there always are. Still, something dramatic is clearly under way and to speak of a new economy is not unreasonable. Indeed, such developments might be interpreted as a third industrial revolution built around what is broadly called information technology. Perhaps some historical perspective is useful, but it is also complicated to make such parallels. How does one compare the impact of the technology that revolutionized the spinning of cotton to that of the personal computer, or the steam engine to the Internet? Can we understand the current restructuring of the modern economy to the lower costs of data processing in the same way we have learned to see the declining cost of output in the textile industry that was the basis of England's fortunes?

The cost of steam power fell dramatically, speeding industrialization more broadly in the eighteenth century. There is already evidence of the same cost-reducing capacities of information technology in our own time. The new processes are analogous to those of the second industrial revolution a century ago when breakthroughs in chemical and mechanical industries, and the impact of electricity and the electric motor on industrial output, vastly changed the nature of production and social life. Today, it can be argued that the growth of information technology—by increasing the speed and lowering the cost of data collection, storage, retrieval, processing, and dissemination through networks that include entertainment and business-to-business channels—is changing our world as dramatically.

David Landes wrote of the first industrial revolution that it "initiated a cumulative, self-sustaining advance in technology whose repercussions would be felt in all aspects of economic life."[22] The same is surely true of the third industrial revolution developments. They too are embodied in capital and work processes, change the balance among class factions, and reconstitute classes and forms of industrial and social organization. There has not however been the liberating end to the "inexorable demands of the clock," as some enthusiasts have suggested. The PC, fax, and cell phone, rather than providing more free time, have enmeshed many in a fast-paced world in which it is far harder to find private, family, or non-work-related communal space. There is exposure to greater speedup and the control over labor processes, and an enlarged, more flexible work force on a global scale has increased inequality everywhere.

Why should we be surprised by the extent of such developments and their widespread impacts? "The bourgeoisie cannot exist without constantly revolutionizing the instruments of production, and without them the whole relations of society," as Marx and Engels wrote in the *Communist Manifesto*. Globalization, which they presciently described in that document, among other places, continues the search for lower waged workers through geographic expansion; this has long been central to the nature of the operation of the capitalist system. Landes writes of early industrialism, "rural manufacturers expanded easily by opening new areas—moving from the environs of the manufacturing towns into nearby valleys, invading less accessible mountain regions, spreading like a liquid seeking its level, in this case the lowest possible wage level. It was in this way that the woollen industry filled the dales of Wiltshire and Somerset and came to thrive all along the Welsh marshes by the end of the sixteenth century."[23] Globalization at the start of the twenty-first century is a continuation of this process on a wider scale.

The price of goods remains, in significant part, a function of economic distance. Economic and political barriers and costs of transport and communication limit dispersion. The factors that play their part today—immigration and emigration, improvements in technology, and forms of labor control—all played their part through the history of capitalism. The pressure of the system's self-expansion dynamic in search of lower cost and greater profit is hardly new. Interpreting the impact of these innovations on the economy is, however, far from a simple matter.

Alan Greenspan, the Federal Reserve System chair, overestimated the essential contribution of information technology in terms of the claims he has made on its ability to reduce uncertainty. It may be true, as he told a March 6, 2000, Boston College Conference on the New Economy, "Before this quantum jump in information availability, most business decisions were hampered by a fog of uncertainty." It is certainly true that control of inventory and material flows across commodity webs that can span many countries, now more closely coordinated in real time, with a better knowledge of consumer preferences on a timely basis and the rest, have cut costs. Yet the basic uncertainty of an anarchic marketplace remains, especially in financial markets where judgments are being made on the basis of discounted future earnings that are unknowable. Investors will continue to cycle between unwarranted optimism and overconfidence and excessive pessimism about future developments, and the business cycle is unlikely to be overcome by new economy technologies.

Whether the world is, at this writing, in the midst of a speculative bubble cannot be known. The software maker Oracle Corporation has a market capitalization greater than the Big Three auto producers; Yahoo! is worth more than Procter & Gamble; and some suggest that Amazon.com should use its sky-high stock to buy up FedEx to deliver its books (even though Amazon has never had a profit and its sales revenues are less than 10 percent of FedEx's revenues). What do we make of these hundreds of startups with a handful of employees each with valuations of hundreds of millions of dollars? Will they be worth billions when they go public? What will their value be a year after that? Some may be another Cisco Company or Lucent, but most will be busts. Indeed, many high fliers may soon become simply commodity producers selling the equivalent of electricity or the phone lines for the standard utilities of the information age, their stock no longer selling at multiples of what for many of them will be modest earnings at best. Moreover the "legacy" economy, the "old" economy, the place where the vast majority continues to work, is in a state of overcapacity and fundamental stagnation. At the start of the twenty-first century many of the high-flying dot-com stocks had crashed, their returns closed down, and some harsh rethinking about the economic properties of hyped self-levitation was under way.

As Marx and Engels understood, capitalism cannot exist without constantly revolutionizing the means of production. It was true in their lifetime and remains true in our own. "The need of a constantly expanding market for its products chases the bourgeoisie over the whole surface of the globe. It must nestle everywhere, settle everywhere, establish connections everywhere. The bourgeoisie has through its exploitation of the world market given a cosmopolitan character to production and consumption in every country." It is not only in our own time that capitalists of the advanced economies have "drawn from under the feet of industry the national ground on which it stood," "destroyed old industries" that were "dislodged by new industries." "In place of the old wants, satisfied by the production of the country, we find new wants, requiring for their satisfaction the products of distant lands and climes. In place of the old local and national seclusion and self-sufficiency, we have intercourse in every direction, universal interdependence of nations." [24]

It is tempting to go on quoting, but the point is clear: the specific forms globalization takes in different epochs differ, but the process of capitalist dynamics is that of dramatic transformations. But these changes are not only beneficial. Crisis and economic collapse are also part of the system's nature, as Soros as well as Marx understands. And yes, those who are so fundamentally affected by these developments, the workers of the world, would probably do well to think about getting together to consider what their societies need to do to make their lives better instead of more precarious by developments in technology and organization. How will these changes affect the condition of the lives of ordinary women and men? Once we consider the role that ordinary women and men come to play in deciding the conditions of their lives through their collective action, we come to the possibilities of a new politics of globalization.

Debating the Politics of Globalization

It is not always easy to see that globalization is also a political process. Capitalism's innovations are normally efficiency enhancing. They raise living standards, on average (although internalizing ecological costs can dramatically change such an equation). This might seem to put them outside the sphere of political contestation. But capitalism innovates and enhances efficiency in ways that typically sacrifice the interests of an entire group of workers who are made obsolete and to whom little or no compensation is paid. While other workers get jobs in the emergent industries, it is less common that displaced workers, especially older ones, do. Much of a generation of workers and often whole communities that depend on their custom for livelihood, wither.

It is not enough to say it would be in the best interests of society in general to offer adequate compensation to these workers. Such compensation may be possible in theory but is never paid, or anywhere near fully paid, in practice. Indeed, if such compensation were mandatory, the form, pace, and impacts of change would be very different. There would be real discussion of how technological changes should be introduced and their social impacts addressed. We must always remember this central aspect of the nature of capitalism—it is always a process of redistributive growth.

The debate is often presented in the form of a stark dichotomy of whether globalization is "good" or "bad." Matters are more complicated, and it is an important task to sort through the intricacies of who globalization is good or bad for, at a given moment, and how it might be made better for those who are paying unacceptably high costs. The operation of the globalization process takes place within, and is mediated by, a set of governance frameworks stretching from the transnational to the local. It is the nature of these institutions, their operation, and the ways they could be restructured that is centrally important. Accepting the free market outcome is not really a possible answer. Markets are always embedded in a larger societal framework. They require social mechanisms to enforce contracts, standards for judging what is permissible behavior by participants. When market outcomes favor a smaller minority and seriously discommode majorities these rules come to be questioned and there are political ramifications that typically produce organizing efforts and movements that eventually change the rules of the game. This has been historically the case. One presumes it will continue to be so.

While some think globalization simply rolls over preexistent norms and preferences, we need to remember that it is the international financial institutions that are imposing the preferred rules of transnational capital for trade and investment. Everyone else is being told they must play by rules that require the cooperation of the governments of the core economies. If the most powerful nations, and we need to remember that this means preeminently the United States, wanted to change things, they could. Many would disagree on this central point. It is often said that even a country as powerful as the United States cannot stand up to the force of global capital markets. For example, it is said that nothing can be done to adequately regulate hedge funds, those vast pools of money managed by speculators. Yet when Long Term Capital Management's 1998 imminent failure was believed to threaten a meltdown of the world financial system, the New York Federal Reserve Bank quickly organized a takeover operation. In this case, intervention was quick to arrive when the health of the haute financiers and the preservation of their well-being were concerned. It would be possible in a different political conjuncture to change rules that allow such high-risk gaming.

It is typically asserted that if we tried to prevent such situations from developing by regulating financial markets, such firms would simply move abroad, to the Bahamas, or some other place where there would hardly be any supervision at all. But this need not be the case. If the United States government ruled that financial firms wishing to do business with United States–based banking institutions had to meet certain standards, they would surely comply. American leadership (and power in the world) would soon prompt international agreement on international regulation. This is exactly how international regulation usually arises. However, such regulation comes first from a consensus within the financial community that regulation is in the best interest of the industry. Only after painful breakdowns take place do regulations that the industry initially opposed as too interventionist come about. It is for this reason, because United States–based capital is so powerfully influential, that the U.S. government chooses not to take actions to tightly regulate offshore venues that transnational capital finds useful (and profitable).

The power of the internationalist sector of the American establishment has grown stronger over time with the deepening globalization
of the economy. United States exports plus imports were equal to 17
percent of our GDP in the 1970s, but more than 25 percent by the 1990s.
Much of this came from parts of the world that were unimportant
sources in earlier times. Both exports and imports dramatically changed
the U.S. economy, in many ways for the better. Exports accounted for a
third of all job growth in the last decades of the twentieth century.
Inexpensive consumer goods from abroad produced lower inflation. The
United States became more focused on holding down taxes and labor
costs. The lesson of the episodes of relative loss of competitiveness—
leading to the 1971 termination of the Bretton Woods system of fixed
exchange rates and the monetary brake-slamming of the early
1980s—was that holding the line on inflation was crucial. The United
States was generally successful at this by holding down wages and
benefits costs. Given such pressures and the ease of global capital
movement, employment security is a central issue of our time.

Companies whipsaw governments everywhere to reduce their
share of taxes (and increase the burden on everyone else). Restoring
the capacity of countries to tax capital is an important step, since so
much of the average citizen's community life comes from publicly
provided goods and services, including the value of public space and
the quality of social life that government helps to create or fails to
provide. The problem is not technical. It is not difficult to conceptu-
alize a unitary tax on corporations, based on worldwide income, that
could be equitably distributed to the countries where company goods
and services are produced and where products are sold. It is politically
difficult because of the power such transnationals exert.

Aims and Perspectives

This book is intended to help us see the present as history, as part of
a process that is subject to pressures of change. One of its themes is that
without historical perspective "globalization" is too easily seen as a new
phenomenon without roots or precedents. A more historical approach
allows us to see that it has been brought into being through complex

processes, which have formed and transformed our ethics, our econo-mies, our history, and our politics.

Within such a historical approach, globalization can also be seen as the outcome of a long tradition in which the presumed superiority of Western culture, modes of thought, and economic organization sup-ported colonialism and imperialism. People were conquered and domi-nated. Their resources were plundered. The governance arrangements were justified—the exploiters were bringing enlightenment to those in darkness, helping to show them the better way. We may laugh today at older rationales ("God made us do it," "the White Man's Burden," and so on), but today's rationales can seem equally implausible and self-serving. The colonial administrators and later anthropologists and other social scientists who provided information about native legal systems and land tenure rules were providing weapons to colonizing forces. Today the administrators and technical advisers to international financial organizations do similar service. This is not the place to review the range of theories developed to support doctrines claiming European colonialism's "scientific" nature, the inevitability and progressiveness of its taking control. It is perhaps enough to say that some of the best minds of the colonial, imperialist, and neocolonialist eras wove impressive rationales for foreign domination. But, we may ask, would we expect less collaboration with the debt regimes of our own time?

Rather than taking for granted the perspectives of our own time, we need to see them in historical context. This book seeks to approach globalization in such a way and to examine its basic assumptions critically. It does not assume that because all citizens have voting rights in capitalist democracies, we all have equal power in shaping the process of globalization. It does not assume that the state is unable to prevent the reshaping of the social and political landscape in accordance with the needs of global markets. Instead it looks at the ways in which the state is active in ensuring the dominance of the markets. It does not assume that technological advance is uniformly beneficial, and that its costs are inflicted on everyone in the same inevitable way. It examines the ways in which the gains and costs of technological and economic change are distributed and how these could be differently or more fairly distributed.

To say that the global village needs a set of rules for all to abide by does not say that these rules are to be the ones preferred by transnational capital, at the expense of workers and the environment. But some set of rules, regulatory structures, and enforcement procedures will be put in place and agreed to so that when foreign capital has disputes with locals there will be a means for their adjudication. To see the present as history is also to see ourselves as being capable of shaping it.

CHAPTER TWO

Consolidating Markets:
From Railroads to Virtual Highways

We see globalization's impact on production and distribution in many spheres of life. New instances present themselves daily. For example, with the launching of Globex—an alliance between Matif, the French exchange, Simex in Singapore, and the Chicago Mercantile Exchange, among other vehicles—the world has twenty-four-hour electronic trading platforms so that anyone with a laptop and a modem may trade financial assets "24/7." There are now many such electronic trading networks. Along with private placements and the work of the private banks that discreetly customize capital movements for the well heeled, these networks make it increasingly difficult to talk about strictly national financial markets. New modes of capital movement obscure the nationality of capital. Such reorganization of markets puts pressure on regulators to remove restrictions to stay competitive and speeds up a potentially dangerous process in which no one is in charge of combating fraud or preventing the contagion effect of panic spreading quickly and uncontrollably.

These are clearly new and significant developments. But it is less clear that they inaugurate a fundamentally new kind of economy. This conclusion—in effect, that we have reached the "end of history," and can no longer learn from the past—may be drawn in triumph or despair. But in both cases it is overly hasty. There are two qualifications that those who are so quick to announce a new age of globalization would do well to consider.

The first qualification concerns the long sweep of the history of capitalism. As Giovanni Arrighi has demonstrated, the fundamental expansion of the 1970s and 1980s does indeed appear to be the predominant tendency of processes of capital accumulation on a world scale. "But it does not appear to be a 'revolutionary' tendency at all," he writes. "Financial expansion of this kind has recurred since the fourteenth century as the characteristic reaction of capital to the intensification of competitive pressures which have invariably ensued from all major expansions of world trade and production."[1] The greater scale and scope of present-day globalization and the power of finance is, as Arrighi says, a continuation of a well-established tendency of the system.

"But surely," it might be argued, "the power of a small group of capitalists, of financiers in New York and London and of international enforcers in Washington, to impose, as if by remote control, constraints on peoples half a world away represents a new stage in capitalist development? Surely, a small group of such men now have greater power than ever before? This is totally unprecedented." That such men exercise extraordinary power is certain. That such relations are so totally new is not. As Fernand Braudel writes: "At this exalted level, a few wealthy merchants in eighteenth-century Amsterdam or sixteenth-century Genoa could throw whole sectors of the European or even the world economy into confusion, from a distance. Certain groups of privileged actors are engaged in circuits and calculations that ordinary people know nothing of. Foreign exchange, for example, which was tied to distance trade movements and to the complicated arrangements of credit, was a sophisticated art."[2]

"But isn't the power of finance capital over the state new?" Political scientists speak of the Westphalian system that for hundreds of years has had rules in which sovereignty is respected and state actors controls what goes on within their territorial boundaries. This system is breaking down under the impact of contemporary globalization. "This," we are told, "is a truly new situation." But as Immanuel Wallerstein has made clear, "Capitalism was from the beginning an affair of the world-economy and not of nation-states." Capital, Wallerstein writes, "has never allowed its aspirations to be determined by national boundaries." [3]

The question of whether the dominance of finance over trade has created a new situation from that known in the past needs to be considered in the context of the discussions of such historians. Consider Arrighi's remark that "In fact, the wealth and power of the Dutch capitalist oligarchy rested more on its control over world financial networks than on commercial networks. . . . As competition in long-distance trade intensified, the Dutch oligarchs could recoup their losses and find a new field of profitable investment in financial speculation. The Dutch capitalist oligarchs therefore had the power to rise above the competition and turn it to its own advantage." [4]

"But surely," you may say, "the Third World debt crises starting in Latin America in the early 1980s is a new phenomenon of our time. It shows the power of international capital acting through new agencies of an emergent world governance structure to force peripheral countries to turn over their wealth." Yes, but neither such debt crises nor the use of debt to force restructuring on dependent social formations is new. Carlos Marichal has written: "That booms and subsequent debt crises have been a permanent feature of Latin American history since independence suggests that there are deep-rooted structural causes which explain their dynamics." [5] He demonstrates how the loan boom gained strength through the export of excess capital from international money markets and crises coincided with widespread downswings of the economies of industrialized nations that provoked sharp and sudden reductions of the outward flow of financial resources precipitating the debt crises of peripheral states. The borrowers are blamed by observers in creditor nations for what today is called "crony capitalism."

The core financier, who is seen by some as helping a less developed economy and making its development possible, can be seen as the oppressor power if we shift the frame somewhat. That "state-creditors actually give nothing away," as Marx wrote, is hardly new. "National debt, i.e., the alienation of the state—whether despotic, constitutional or republican—marked with its stamp the capitalist era . . . As with the stroke of the enchanter's wand, [public debt] endows barren money with the power of breeding and thus turns it into capital, without the necessity of its exposing itself to the troubles and risks inseparable from its employment in industry or even in usury."[6] Public debt, and its twin, taxation, play key roles in the oppression of the working class. From Marx's perspective "overtaxation" is not "an incident, but rather a principle." He wrote of "[t]he great part that the public debt, and the fiscal system corresponding to it, has played in the capitalisation of wealth and the expropriation of the masses."[7]

It has also been said that in the age of globalization the rule of finance has replaced gunboat diplomacy, the use of the marines, the old imperialism. Yet two objections can be raised against the argument that this makes it fundamentally new and different. The first is that women and children are bombed by the U.S. military in such places as Iraq and Serbia because our government wants these governments to change their policies. If this is not gunboat diplomacy, it is surely guided missile diplomacy. There is an active willingness on the part of the United States, often in opposition to world opinion, to intervene with great violence to attempt to get its way. Second, as readers of the history of British imperialism are well aware, finance was always an instrument of control. Karl Polanyi reminds us that "The Pax Britannica held sway sometimes by the ominous poise of heavy ship's cannon, but more frequently it prevailed by the timely pull of a thread in the international monetary network."[8] Finance, as he points out, "acted as a powerful moderator in the councils and policies of a number of smaller sovereign states. Loans, and the renewal of loans, hinged upon credit, and credit upon good behavior."[9] Polanyi describes how the influence of *haute finance* was ensured through its unofficial administration of the finances of vast semicolonial regions of the world in the age of classic imperialism and how currency "has become the pivot of national politics" in the years in which the gold standard came under final assault.

In sum, those who suggest that some historical break is currently taking place in world capitalist development do not seem to be on firm ground. Harry Magdoff writes: "The desire and need to operate on a world scale is built into the economics of capitalism. Competitive pressures, technical advances, and recurring imbalances between productive capacity and effective demand create continuous pressures for the expansion of markets. The risks and uncertainties of business, interrelated with the unlimited acquisitive drive for wealth, activate the entrepreneur to accumulate even greater assets and, in the process, to scour every corner of the earth for new opportunities. What stand in the way," Magdoff writes, "in addition to technical limits of transportation and communication, are the recalcitrance of natives and the rivalry of other capitalist nation states."[10]

In our own time the continuing operating imperatives of the system, and how its contradictions produce crisis, how rivalries are played out, and the resistance these developments engender are not so very different. The point of a systemic analysis is to see the structural relations between core and periphery in terms of relative power, the cyclical instability of capitalism as a system, and how both evolve in terms of international finance and debt relations. Of course each new episode is unique. But each is a reflection as well of a deeper structure.

The continuities between past and present lie not only at the level of the deep structures of capitalism. Within the constraints of these structures, far-reaching changes in the organization of economy and society take place. Globalization in our time represents such a change, but the nature of the change is by no means unprecedented. For the present can be interpreted by comparing it historically to the transition—roughly a hundred years ago—in which regional capitals and economic areas formerly distinct were transformed into a single national market in the United States. At that time the U.S. economy was transformed from its regional markets and pre-mass-production economy to a national economy. Today there is an analogous movement from national economies to a globalized economic system based on a new constellation of leading sectors, internationalized statist institutions, and emergent class structures.

This analogy is developed here by examining the importance of mergers and economic restructuring, the ideological characterization of these developments, the role of the financiers, and the alternative responses on offer from various quarters of the ruling class. Such a historical parallel allows us to see the underlying continuity in the way capitalism as a system operates, as well as how the particularities of a period and the political choices societies make influence the trajectory of their society as part of the larger system.

From Railroads to Virtual Highways:
Parallels with the Economy of a Century Ago

At the start of the new millennium, the typical American is over-whelmed by larger forces of economic restructuring whose significance are not clear, and which seem to dwarf human agency. In recent decades intellectuals have implicitly theorized the present as a period of transition: as post-industrial, post-modern and so on. In much the same way, the United States from the end of Reconstruction to the outbreak of World War I has been repeatedly described as being in a period of transition, experienced "as if individual human beings had gone underground and the national scene had been taken over by vast economic movements." [11]

As Daniel Boorstin writes, the period of the 1870s, 1880s, and early 1890s appeared as an "in-between" age "when great events were supposedly not happening but only being prepared." Such a description has a certain resonance comparable to the intellectual mood a century later with a similar feeling that an age had passed but it was not yet clear what would be next. An even closer parallel exists with Richard DuBoff's assertion: "The paradox of the last third of the nineteenth century is that it was a Golden Age—the heyday of private enterprise if ever there was one—and yet a period of profound instability and anxiety." [12] "Something very similar can surely be said about the last third of the twentieth century, again a heyday of private enterprise but a period of great anxiety as well. Globalization has put pressure on workers the same way the emergence of the national economy did a century earlier. These transformations as capitalism moves into new stages of its development are profoundly unsettling.

Accounts of the final decades of the United States in the final decades of the nineteenth century and the global economy in the final decades of the twentieth century capture something more specific than the ordinary upheavals of capitalism: the consolidation of new and larger markets. A century or more ago, the average American, whether a farmer, merchant, or craft worker, could contrast the past with the uncertain present, a situation characterized by "the transition from relatively stable, local business affairs to intense nationwide competition that rendered his way of making a living less secure." [13] Today the analogous transition is from the experience of the dominance of large-scale national production and that of industrial workers, which had prevailed since the turn of the century, to the uncertainties imposed by an encroaching globalism.

A century ago, as in our own time, there were revolutionary developments in communication and transportation that led to the enlarged scope of markets and the restructuring of production and control to match the new possibilities. In the late nineteenth century, it was the telegraph and the railroad that linked more tightly distant groups and sections of the economy into one interdependent nation, so that by 1914 the United States was a dramatically different place. It is likely that by 2014 the changes evident at the turn of the new century will have as fully transformed the United States and the global unit will be recognized as the dominant one for economic analysis. Just as the regions of this country were not isolated before the emergence of the national market, and that this development qualitatively changed the nature of their connectedness, so too globalization is affecting nation-states.

The railroad boom was the vehicle for the transformation allowing the movement of goods and people, and railroads were the first giant corporations. Given their size they dominated the economy. Their existence permitted changed consumption and production patterns. It is in these years that futures markets developed for corn, hogs, and other commodities and speculative trading activities took off. A century later, the computer industry provides the cheap movement of information and the processing power to change consumption and production patterns from customized web shopping to online bidding by corporate suppliers, and real-time communication that is transforming our world. In each instance the improved mode of communication allowed greater certainty concerning events and markets. The immediacy of transmitting orders and instructions allowed control of activities in remote location tying them more closely together and increasing the potential size of the market. They also allow for financial instruments, derivatives of all kinds, to be traded electronically on exchanges led by those in Chicago with their century-plus experience in agricultural futures. And just as we are seeing consolidation of exchanges today with cross-border mergers to make the buying and selling of stocks, bonds, and other financial instruments a lower-cost proposition, centralizing the centers of capital, we may note that in 1850 the United States had 250 stock exchanges. The telegraph and tickertape reduced their number dramatically at the expense of smaller regional markets. The computer and telecom cost reduction in trading in the present era is having a similar impact on a global scale.

A century ago, groups of farmers and workers protested the vast and growing power of monopolies. They did not accept economic science, which claimed that by forming unions and trying to increase wages they were interfering with the market and could only do more harm than good. Nor did they accept the courts' declaration that collective action by working people—but not collusion by corporations—was an illegal restraint of trade. Farmers told to raise less corn and more hell did so, not only protesting but electing populists as governors and senators, defeating the two parties of big business.

Working people looked for allies as they sought to create anti-systemic identities. Over the course of the nineteenth century, working men's associations changed their conception of self from a vision of themselves as "producers"—aligned with other productive classes such as skilled craftsmen and manufacturers, against "nonproducing" bankers, lawyers, and land speculators—to a new collective identity as workers. In the twentieth century, the conceptualization of workers as the male blue-collar, industrial proletariat ossified into an understanding of the working class, which by century's end had become problematic and counterproductive for the alliances necessary to effect fundamental social change. Just as in the presence of industrialism the then new collective identity of "workers" had allowed a revolutionary politics to develop, in the twenty-first century globalization requires the conceptualization of a collective identity on the part of any revolutionary movement that is germane to its context.

The difficulties that race, ethnicity, and space created for radical politics in industrial economies in the late nineteenth and twentieth centuries continue into the present. But a further substantial obstacle to unity was the emerging division within the working class between blue-collar constituencies and those who did white-collar work and had professional aspirations, which were understood to be separate from and often in opposition to the industrial proletariat. Geographical separation, the growth of suburbs, as well as class recomposition, with the growth of new layers of knowledge workers, technical professionals, and managerial workers, affected politics everywhere. Globalization reshuffles the cards further by creating coalitions among those who understand their own interests to be in opposition to, and those who see themselves as benefiting from, its dynamics.

To suggest such a parallel is not to imagine that nothing has changed over the past century, for everything changes constantly, but rather to insist that developments can be understood in terms of patterns that tie past transformation to current and future ones even as we also study each historical conjuncture in terms of its uniqueness. There are patterns in capitalist accumulation that make contemporary trends more readable, comprehensible in terms of the ways capitalist accumulation and the development of the forces of production have historically been developed.

Mergers and Markets

At the end of the twentieth century, as at the end of the nineteenth, consolidation in older industries to remove excess capacity and to better position companies to compete with rivals unleashed powerful merger movements. Even the financial press, which daily reported on the extensive scope of the mergers, especially cross-border alliances, is today subject to the same pressures. So that Dow Jones (itself just over a century old), the U.S. publisher of business news and information (and the owner of the *Wall Street Journal*) agreed to swap shareholdings and collaborate with George von Holzbrinck, publisher of the German business paper *Handelsblatt,* and had plans for new European printing sites from Italy to Scandinavia. Another cross-border merger, between the Pearson Group (owner of the *Financial Times*) and a German publisher controlled by Bertelsmann, another media giant, to launch a German-language business newspaper may have motivated the action in much the same way that auto and oil companies, book publishers, and banks had sought out partners in an effort to "bulk up" for the intense competition in which presence in the key markets was requisite to survival.

The consolidation of U.S. industry was most rapid between 1897 and 1904—in those years 4,277 firms were consolidated into 257. The hundred largest quadrupled in size and took control of 40 percent of the country's industrial capacity in a process called "Morganization," since so many of these consolidations took place under the control of J. P. Morgan. Morgan stressed the increased efficiencies, economies of scale and administrative rationalizations that they permitted and the order they brought. Critics called this monopolization, initiated so as to profit from control over output and pricing. Jean Strouse, one of Morgan's biographers, contrasts his view of what he was doing with those of his critics in the following terms:

> Combination, monopoly, mergers, consolidation, trust: to Morgan and his colleagues, these forms of industrial organization made practical and financial sense. They had grown out of new mass-production and distribution capacities that were radically reducing operating costs, increasing efficiency, and creating immense national wealth. Elsewhere in America, however, the new industrial leviathans' subjugation of labor, stifling of free market competition, and concentration of financial and political power were widely seen as a threat to the country's fundamental ideals.[14]

It depended on one's viewpoint. Those who looked from the top saw a more prosperous and well-ordered economy. Those looking up from the base of the pyramid and who were exploited by corporate power understood the reorganization of the political economy differently. The political establishment tended to be partial to the Morgan perspective even if some opposed him and others were not averse to making headlines criticizing Morgan, perhaps the most hated man in America.

Morgan's greatest achievement was the 1901 formation of U.S. Steel (as a holding company in New Jersey), the nation's first billion-dollar corporation, capitalized at the equivalent of 7 percent of the Gross National Product that year, at a time when the entire federal budget was 350 million dollars. Ron Chernow writes: "The genesis of United States Steel in 1901 was inseparable from the permissive regulatory mood, which followed the 1900 GOP landslide." [15] Yet this permissive period was also one of mass resistance to the monopolies and a political backlash against Morgan and his allies.

Just as a hundred years ago the giant industrial corporations that were to dominate the U.S. economy for most of the coming century—the likes of U.S. Steel and Standard Oil—were formed in breathtaking mergers, so today we may well be seeing the basis of the twenty-first century economy being created. Of the twenty-five largest American corporations in 1960, only four are still on the list at the start of the new millennium. Similar changes are taking place globally as old industries fade and their space is taken by new ones prominent in the cyber economy —Nokia in Finland, Ericsson in Sweden, and others. The U.K. firm Vodafone was not yet two decades old when it swallowed Mannesmann, which in one form or another has been around for over a century, in the largest merger ever and the first hostile merger in Germany by a foreign firm. The struggle to dominate the terrain of the new economy is accelerating.

There is little doubt that computers, software, and other information technology products, which together accounted for 40 percent of all business investment in the United States in 1999, are remaking the global political economy. More books are sold online than in bookstores. New car buyers flock to the Internet while dealers fight back through state franchise laws. But when you can buy a car in Montana from a website in Delaware for delivery in New Mexico it is hard to see how such tactics can stall the emergence of e-commerce's expansion into just about any conceivable market. On the other hand, just as in earlier waves of capitalist expansion, maximization of private profit collides with not only social need in the ways in which technologies are developed but serve capital in many ways at the expense of working people. The trajectory is toward monopoly, duopoly, or oligopoly for most markets from telecom to banking, from soft drinks to fast food. Reform also follows certain historical patterns and the contestations a century ago over how finance should be regulated have lessons for our own time.

In the nineteenth century the United States experienced recurrent financial crises as banks failed, people lost their jobs and their savings, and the economy plunged into recession/depression. After initially resisting social control, the banks finally accepted government supervision of the money supply and of banking, but were able to shape the form such institutionalization took so that it worked in their interests.

As global financial regulatory institutions evolve we can expect that they will follow the pattern of national-level regulation of the banks. The creation of the Federal Reserve System in the United States in 1913 was—as the historian Ron Chernow writes—"in many ways a Morgan godsend."[16] Real financial power remained with Wall Street but the Fed took the limelight. The first occupant of the key position in the new arrangement, the governor of the New York Federal Reserve Bank, Benjamin Strong, "had Morgan written all over his resumé." The House of Morgan in New York sent Strong to their English partner in London "for tutorials on how the bank [of England] operated. Through Strong's influence, the Federal Reserve System would prove far more of a boon than a threat to Morgan. The New York Fed and the Bank would share a sense of purpose such that the House of Morgan would be known on Wall Street as the Fed Bank. So, contrary to expectations, frustrated reformers only watched Morgan's power grow after 1913."[17] In the same way the great international banks of our time have used the IMF as their collection agency, gaining strength and accumulating power from the way regulation has been made to work. J. P. Morgan was the Federal Reserve and IMF of his time. He defended sound finance and prevented capital flight by arranging lines of credit in time of panic. His agents shaped U.S. foreign policy. Chernow writes of the "explicit fusion of financial and government power. In time it would become hard to disentangle the House of Morgan from various aspects of Anglo-American policy." He writes of this mutually advantageous alliance: "Washington wanted to harness the new financial power to coerce foreign governments into opening their markets to American goods or adopting pro-American policies. The banks, in turn, needed levers to force debt repayment and welcomed the government's police powers in distant places."[18]

In the 1920s, Morgan partner Thomas Lamont talking about fascist Italy sounded much like Milton Friedman talking about Chilean dictatorship a half-century later and the host of financiers talking about authoritarian governments in East Asia in the early 1990s. "In public appearances, Lamont tried to deflect attention from Mussolini's politics to his economic record. Wall Street enjoyed pretending there were two Mussolinis—the sound economic leader and the tough politician—

who could be treated separately. Mussolini spouted the predictable litany of promises—balanced budgets, low inflation, and sound money—that bankers adored. Resorting to sophistry, Lamont said he was only praising the Italian economy, not Mussolini or fascism." [19]

In a similar manner today, Morgan's heirs move the money stolen by dictators from their people to safe havens while using the U.S. government and the global state economic institutions as collection agencies. They also finance, through junk bonds and other forms of excessive leverage, the growing concentration and centralization of economic power.

The Emergent Monopolists of the New Economy

Ten days into the new millennium the shape of things to come emerged with the announcement that America Online was purchasing Time Warner in the (then) largest merger ever, valued at $153 billion. What was so surprising was that an upstart firm such as AOL, which had one-fifth the revenues and 15 percent of the workforce of Time Warner, was buying one of the oldest and largest publishing and enter-tainment empires in the world. Before the deal Time Warner stock sold at fourteen times its earnings but AOL traded at fifty-five times its earnings. Since AOL was "worth" nearly twice as much as Time Warner as their stock was valued in the marketplace, they could use it as currency. When Yahoo! first sold stock to the public in the spring of 1986 and these shares skyrocketed (the company was valued by Wall Street at $800 million—then an astounding sum, but a tiny fraction of what its market valuation would soon become)—a new economy was created. Investors confident that the new media was transforming the economy went crazy bidding up valuations that have continued to rise at an unbelievable rate.

In 1993, AOL had half a million subscribers, and paid Time Warner half a million dollars to put *Time* magazine on line. Time Warner could have bought AOL quite easily, but did not. In late 1996, AOL had figured out that rather than pay Time Warner for content, it could charge Time Warner for the exposure it got through AOL's portal to the Internet and its millions of subscribers. Eight years after AOL shares first sold to the public to the time of the merger AOL stock prices rose 50,000 percent. AOL's value had soared with other dot-coms expected to turn huge profits in the new Internetted world. This optimistic expectation allowed them to trade shares of their high-flying stock for ownership of the lower valued Time Warner in the largest merger in history. If AOL had not acted when it did, and new technologies had emerged that made its dial-up phone connection to the Internet obsolete (broadband, much faster and capacious cable connections, or wireless fiberoptics options now in development), it might well have been the acquired not the acquirer.

This merger is of interest here not so much in terms of who buys whom. It is rather the process of consolidation and the implications of emergent power that is important. The merger brings together the cable outlets owned by Time Warner, once prized for their television capacity but now seen as routes for better Internet connectivity with their vast "content"—movies from Warner Brothers and New Line Cinema, Warner Brothers Music, TV networks CNN, HBO, TBS, TNT, and WB, and a vast publishing empire. Investors who owned AOL initially reacted badly to the announced merger because the new giant would not grow as fast as AOL had been able to as a small fleet-footed dot-com. The people putting the merger together saw the cross-sales potential and were aware that if they did not pursue the alliance, others would and their companies would lose out in the not-so-long term as consolidations changed the nature of Internet-media economics. Soaring market values allow consolidations, as they have in every other period of concentration in American capitalism's history, creating the monopolies that dominate the political economy for many decades.

In the infancy of a new sector, the unknowable future can look rosy enough to seem to justify such valuations; as time passes real achievement is required. One way to profit is to control some highly regarded technology or essential component of a value chain. Microsoft's Windows system, for example, as the operating system used by 90 percent of computers, is such a lock, and it is the company's actions in tying other products to it that the government found to be preventing competition in the industry. AOL, learning from the Microsoft case, promises open access, allowing·other companies use of its cable TV lines. It hopes that its own wide array of offerings will hold consumers, and of course the manner in which it provides such access may be viewed as unfair. Indeed, some critics see such power to control so much of the content and shopping as the end of competition on the Internet. Canadian officials have already announced they are considering loosening rules that now require a certain proportion of Canadian content for radio and TV broadcasters because new products delivered via the Internet from U.S. competitors (they speak specifically of the new AOL Time Warner) would put their own companies at a disadvantage if they had to follow current local content rules. Commercialization of the Internet on American terms means Americanization of the Internet.

The issues of monopoly power and the need for anti-trust action that were so central a part of American reaction to the "new economy" as the nineteenth century changed to the twentieth century and a truly national economy emerged were evident as the twentieth century became the twenty-firstand globalization concerns became a central issue. The specific nature of the market control issues may be different, given the technologies involved, but whether we discuss railroads or the information highway, the similarities are clear.

Seeking Monopoly Power

The U.S. government once argued that Microsoft's web browser unfairly challenged Netscape. Now Netscape is part of AOL, which has merged into the much larger AOL Time Warner. Today it is Microsoft that is at a relative disadvantage in the race to dominate the Internet, yet it still faces a breakup at the hands of the Justice Department, reminding us of the similar breakup that Standard Oil—also found guilty of monopolization—endured a century or so earlier. Just weeks after AOL Time Warner merger, the company announced it would acquire EMI and merge it with Warner Music to create the world's largest record company. This new company would sell one in four records bought in the United States. More of these sales in the future will be downloaded over the Internet, dramatically changing the nature of the industry as online music replaces CDs in the same way CDs, to a great extent, replaced records and tapes.

Within a month of the AOL Time Warner announcement, it was no longer the largest merger in history. Vodafone, a British-based wireless communications company, after some maneuvering bought control of Mannesmann in a $183 billion takeover. This was the first hostile cross-national takeover of a major German firm. The German corporatist model had never before allowed such a thing. The German government had always protected "its" companies. Yet this time the government did nothing. After all, Daimler-Benz had recently taken control of Chrysler. Could it have different rules for "German" companies? I put quotation marks around "German" because non-Germans, mostly U.S. and British institutional investors, already owned 60 percent of Mannesmann's stocks. The internationalization of finance and the adoption of the euro have undercut the nationalist economic model, which the European transnationals have outgrown.

The Vodafone merger was an effort to create European, and then global, market dominance. The company will offer the same kind of multimedia access that AOL Time Warner will, but through a wireless delivery system (whereas the U.S. firm would use desktop computers and TV sets). It is possible these rivals will see the advantage of joining forces at some point to monopolize the delivery-and-content-providing alternatives. That there will be continued jockeying first—Vodafone has alliances with IBM, Sun Microsystems, Ericsson, Nokia and others already—to build Internet service capabilities. Some of these companies have alliances with AOL as well.

The monopoly potential of these industrial convergences comes from what economists call network externalities. There is an incentive to use the same technology for multiple purposes, and the greater the number of people who use the technological standard, the more attractive it is for others to use it. Once a video format becomes dominant, it becomes economical for everyone to use that format. The tendency toward monopoly is inherent in such externalities. That is why products like web browsers are given away to build up a large usership. Later, companies can sell updated versions of its product to users, who are already hooked on the standard, and can make money by attracting advertisers that want to reach this user group.

The dynamics of technology and the creative evolution of economic control strategies cannot, of course, be predicted. Nokia, currently continental Europe's most highly valued company, is moving to set up its own mobile portal to control access to the Internet. If it succeeds, given its current technology advantages in wireless communication, it could edge AOL out. It is also possible that chips developed by Intel and others could, at very low cost, turn all wireless phones into high-efficiency products, as good as the top Nokia phones. This would turn cell phones into low-margin commodity products rather than rent-earning, proprietary, cutting-edge technology able to dominate access to the Internet. Similarly, instead of remaining the conqueror, Vodafone could become a mere wireless pipeline, one of many Internet portals controlling the profitable end of tomorrow's cyber economy. The quest for monopoly power is fiercely competitive. No one knows the specific path it will take.

Technology has a central role to play in determining which companies come out on top, but there should be little doubt that there will be both consolidations and monopoly profits made or that new technologies will continue to revolutionize the economic contours of global capitalism. One can point to the prospects of fiber-optics systems— which can split single strands of light into dozens of strands of light, each channeling the equivalent of hundreds of telephone calls—shaking things up, and reshuffling who captures the monopoly profits in the new interconnected cyber-economy world. Cisco Systems, already among the half-dozen most valuable corporations in the world, is spending billions buying startups in the fiber-optics field in hope of dominating this new technological frontier. It has rivals in Nortel and Lucent. Which of these names will become the familiar household equivalents of Ford, McDonald's, and Coke in the twenty-first century economy remains to be seen.

Opportunity matrices change fast; indeed, at web speed. New technologies suddenly loom as effective alternatives. Old norms are roadkill. It is this dynamism of capitalism that suggests that it remains a revolutionary mode of production with new possibilities yet unexplored. And it is this dynamism that makes it difficult for critics to do anti-systemic organizing. Yet the need for democratic governance over capital's accumulation drive remains as strong as it has ever been as the capacity of capitalism to exploit and control grows dramatically in the cyber stage of its development.

Colonizing the Mind: Power in the New Economy

The cost of the way capitalist social relations develop the forces of production produces deep social contradictions. The Internet-related technologies are hardly an exception. In the age of cyberspace capitalism we face a new kind of technological determinism, which says these developments are inevitable. Governments and social movements that attempt to resist will only fail or mess up the "freedom" the Internet promises with harmful and inefficient regulation. The same arguments that were once given against those who would regulate working hours and conditions during the industrial revolution—and are given again today to extending such protections globally—are offered to protect the freedom of the Internet, to keep its transactions from being taxed, and to prevent its abuses of consumer privacy becoming subject to social regulation. Technology policies are political by nature. Corporations want to set the policies and deny a role to the public. If we do not want to see uncontested corporate domination of this increasingly important piece of the global political economy, and do not wish to be manipulated by corporations using these new technologies, there must be a change in consciousness, awareness, and organization of political resistance. The mergers between AOL and Time Warner, Vodafone and Mannesmann, and other concentrations within the globalized Internetted economy, represent a shaping of the twenty-first-century political economy that must be met with the same sort of popular anger and mass mobilization that earlier efforts to monopolize provoked. The workers of the world need to unite on many fronts, including cyberspace.

CHAPTER THREE

State Power in the World Economy: From National Keynesianism to Neoliberalism

Much of the anger of the demonstrators in Seattle and elsewhere was directed at global financial institutions, such as the WTO, that act on behalf of global corporations. In this context, the state appears to play a lesser role. However, it would be a mistake to view the state as powerless within the global economy. Rather, state power has been consciously remade in such a way as to serve the interests of corporations rather than citizens. In this process, the social democratic national Keynesianism, which was predominant since the Second World War, has made way for global neoliberalism. In order to understand the role of the state within the process of globalization today, we need to return to the making of national Keynesianism, and examine its rise and fall.

The origins of national Keynesianism are to be found in the economic developments of the interwar years. The international trade and finance policies pursued in those years by the Anglo-American governments bear a striking resemblance to those we see in the global neoliberalism of our own time. The important international gatherings of the interwar years, such as the Genoa Conference of 1922, when they dealt with international financial questions, called for an end to "futile and mischievous" exchange controls and demanded greater independence for central banks and less political interference in international finance. Of course, commission members were themselves leading figures from the world of high finance representing the major powers whose bankers, often these same men, dominated global money markets. The Finance Commission at the Genoa Conference was chaired, for example, by the British Chancellor of the Exchequer. After the Second World War, the senior American representative played the dominant role. In each instance, the idea was to enhance the role of the free market, a strategy motivated by the interests of the strongest participants in those markets. Markets were not then, nor have they ever been, "free" in the sense that ideological partisans have argued they were and can be.

An important construct in the mythology of the free market is the idea that the gold standard worked automatically and efficiently to create a smoothly adjusting international financial order over a large part of the nineteenth century. This idea has been shown to be historically inaccurate. In fact, the gold standard came into effect as the basis for Western European international monetary affairs only in the 1870s and didn't spread to the greater part of the world until century's end. It depended on very specific economic and political circumstances, which could not be re-created once the working class came onto the scene and was represented in the parliaments of the core states by its own political parties. Once workers understood and were in a position to act on the tradeoff between employment and balance of payments, convertibility above all other goals became politically too costly.

Further, as interimperialist rivalries grew, British hegemony declined, and the financial cooperation needed to make the system work became less likely. The Great Depression dramatically eroded the power of financial orthodoxy and the material interests it represented. But the success of social democratic parties and governments and the growth period of the postwar era, along with the decline of rank-and-file militancy, aided by the anti-communism of the Cold War period and encroaching globalization pressures, allowed finance capital to regain the upper hand.

In the last years of the 1920s—as in the 1990s—the United States economy was on a long cyclical expansion while much of the rest of the world was in recession/depression. Capital-short nations tried to export their way out of crisis, protectionism increased, debt burdens became heavier, defaults grew more numerous, and the financial system fell apart. Calls for austerity as the only "realistic" solution made matters worse. Peripheral economies with inadequate reserves suspended debt payment as capital flight worsened. At the end of the 1920s stability at the center was undermined. The United States went into crisis and extended depression. Industrial production fell 48 percent between 1929 and 1932 as our speculative bubble collapsed.

National Keynesianism was itself a reaction to the pain of the Great Depression and so a rejection of the earlier orthodoxy of free markets or laissez-faire economics. The Great Depression had shaken the confidence of the ruling class and raised basic questions about the stability of unregulated capitalism. On the Continent, industrialists had collaborated with the fascists while communists and socialists had been active in the resistance to Nazism. At the end of the war, labor and the Left had high prestige and the organized political strength to be a major force in postwar governance. The social democratic corporatist state that emerged, and the enlarged welfare emphasis, was a measure of this support and an indication of the concessions necessary to prevent anti-capitalist movements from taking power. National Keynesianism provided the basis for a structure of governance in which the state promotion of profit growth and higher living standards coexisted. National champions were protected and subsidized, capital controls retained. In Japan and later other East Asian nations, a corporatism without labor emerged under more authoritarian political conditions. They pursued state-led development with the different constellation of class forces prevalent in these economies. The economic strategy of income distribution and safety net provisions defined the economic role of the state in Europe and to a lesser extent in the United States in the decades after the Second World War until at least sometime in the late 1960s.

The Erosion of the National Keynesian State

The growing power of international capital markets eroded the national Keynesian strategy of income distribution and safety net provisions. In time, it produced pressure on the state at all levels, national, regional and local, to adopt neoliberal forms of organization. This process of erosion became increasingly evident from the late 1960s, when the economies of Western Europe and Japan having recovered from wartime devastation offered increased competition in global markets. Because the Cold War organized consciousness in terms of an east-west Manichean conflict, it took a while to see that former enemies as well as allies had become economic competitors. Capital accumulation led to concentration and centralization of economic power and corporations outgrew their local economies and sought to expand beyond their national borders. United States–based transnational capital led, followed by those of other core nations, accompanied by the growth of international finance. As capital sought the freedom of mobility on a world scale, the material basis of national Keynesianism was undermined as the political alliance of corporatism in Europe and the Democratic party's liberal-labor hegemonic coalition in the United States split apart. Global capital sought freedom to invest, market, and produce on a planetary scale.

Fortunately for the United States, conjunctural events in both Germany and Japan undercut the competitiveness of these rivals. German reunification was extremely costly. The fixing of too high a par value for the East German currency in terms of the West German one, and the dismantling of the East's organizational infrastructure, accentuated a dependency that would prove immensely costly to taxpayers—a seemingly perpetual transfer of about five percent of GDP—which had the impact of reducing German competitiveness. The par value set for the German mark in its fixed relation to the euro in a similar manner overvalued the currency and intensified pressure on wages and benefits. Germany's labor laws and social spending were blamed for a profit squeeze.

Japan, which had led the world in economic growth to the point of challenging the United States for economic preeminence in the 1980s, was unable to reinvest its growing surpluses productively, a problem intensified by an irresponsible macroeconomic policy of maintaining low interest rates as a way of encouraging the purchase of United States financial assets by Japanese investors. The result was serious overinvestment due to the artificially low cost of capital. Continued state guarantees to highly leveraged corporations and banks fed a speculative asset bubble in stock prices and property values that could not be sustained. As rich as Japan was, it could ill afford a decade of stagnation in the aftermath of the bubble bursting.

In contrast, the reorganization of the resurgent American economy was led by the financial sector, which ruthlessly wrung value out of a restructuring of U.S. capitalism. There were "lean and mean" reorganizations that downsized corporations with massive layoffs and plant closings—activities that were less feasible in Japan and Europe due to more paternalistic social contracts, but which provided precedents that emboldened these capitalist classes to emulate U.S. practices. At the same time there was growth of information processing, software, revolutionary telecom innovation, and media in which America's new economy excelled. These sectors burst onto the American scene in a development that argued for the superiority of the American form of entrepreneurial capitalism, but the more regulated and the statist regulatory regimes in Europe and Asia resisted a process that could also be characterized as creative destruction. In these countries, people were less eager to sacrifice their socialized medicine, longer vacations, better working conditions, and employment and retirement security. Yet the material and ideological onslaught of neoliberal globalization had its impact as it became more costly to defend corporatist arrangements and the more internationalized sectors of national capital everywhere moved away from the national Keynesian accommodations that they had accepted in the post–Second World War period for conjunctural reasons.

Technological developments facilitated this growth as the cost of information transmission and processing and transportation costs fell. International capital markets developed rapidly, aided by the power of computers to do the complex calculations and data manipulations to price financial derivatives and track trades. The FIRE—finance, insurance, real estate—sector contributes more by conventional national income accounting standards than manufacturing to U.S. GDP, producing income for the upper end of the income distribution and increasing inequality worldwide, while contributing to instability and producing uncertainties for the "real" economy. This effect may be a significant part of the explanation for the slowdown of global economic growth since financial liberalization. While increasing allocative efficiency in a static sense, the financial sector's propensity to overshoot reinforces and amplifies cycles.

The growth of finance has strengthened the U.S. economy and the profit picture of its banks and other financial institutions. Because the United States absorbs so much of world savings, at this writing two-thirds of the total, it has been able to live beyond its means, running up a huge current account balance-of-payments deficit. The huge profitability derived from finance has encouraged U.S. policy makers, especially the Treasury Department, which dominates the executive branch and runs on a bankers' logic, to lean heavily on finance ministers around the world. The U.S. Treasury has been a leader in orienting global economic restructuring in a direction that is at the same time highly profitable for the United States–based financial sector and destabilizing and costly to much of the rest of the world. A central aspect, perhaps the central aspect, of globalization has been financial liberalization.

The centrality of the dollar as the global reserve currency gave the American economy important advantages. The United States could run a huge balance of payments deficit, funding consumption that exceeded domestic production and investment that outstripped domestic savings, because foreigners were willing to build up dollar holdings. The robustness of globalized capital markets was a major factor in the growing strength of the United States economy. American banks were the leaders and the greatest profiteers from the deregulation of finance. London had traditionally been the world financial center and had a continuing comparative advantage in this sector. U.K. banks also greatly benefited from the dramatic growth in financial services.

These contingent events and other unique happenings in various nations, from the Latin American debt crisis to the demise of Soviet Communism, can be seen in a larger context: the shift from a national Keynesian social structure of accumulation in the postwar years to a regime of global neoliberalism emerging in the closing years of the 1970s. In this process, the economic role of the state came to be redirected. The integrative functions for many governments are no longer central as communities are reorganized based on relations with the global system. Those individuals and groups who are seen as not contributing to the globalized order and/or who have lost political leverage find their citizenship rights challenged and entitlements diminished or denied. The state "container" remains but its function becomes increasingly a disciplinary one as the policies of governments are reoriented to serve globalization functions on behalf of transnational capital.

U.S. Global Power and the Rise of the Global Financial Institutions

To understand the changing role of state power in the process of globalization, we need also to understand three global institutions that have become increasingly prominent in the postwar world and are being structured to take on greater "stateness," the characteristics of global governance serving the interests of transnational corporations and international finance. These institutions are the World Trade Organization (WTO), the International Monetary Fund (IMF), and the World Bank (WB).

The IMF and the WB were created in 1944 by the United States and the United Kingdom, with others invited to endorse and join without being able to play much of a role in designing the rules of these clubs. The IMF was charged with overseeing exchange rate stability by lending to nations who were in short-term need of funds to balance their accounts. The WB, actually the World Bank Group since it contains a number of separate facilities that lend to developing countries under a range of conditions and interest rates to support projects, was then the International Bank for Reconstruction and Development and charged with aiding European postwar recovery.

The WTO was established in 1995, but its roots go back to the late 1940s when an effort spearheaded by the executive branch of the United States government working with its British counterparts proposed the creation of an International Trade Organization that other nations would be invited to join. At it turned out, the U.S. Congress, dominated by isolationists and representatives of national capital suspicious of the internationalist orientation of the proposed organization, feared that sovereignty would be lost and would not allow America to join. A stopgap General Agreement on Tariffs and Trade (GATT) was institutionalized and served as a weaker instrument until, by the 1990s, the internationalist wing of the American political establishment was strong enough to gain congressional support for the WTO.

These Bretton Woods institutions have "morphed" into stronger instrumentalities of governance. They direct the economic policies and demand changes in domestic institutions from those who would seek their aid to a far greater extent than in the past. The basic thrust of their policies has not changed in any important way. They have responded to the United States desire to open markets everywhere to American penetration. Economic weakness has allowed a wedge for United States coercion. For example, in 1947, when the United States insisted that the British restore convertibility, a prostrate U.K. had little choice. This turned out to be a disaster for the British. Fifty years later, during the Asian financial crisis, the United States again insisted that high interest rates were the solution, so that creditors would not take losses yet still maintain confidence. The insistence that convertibility must be maintained in order to placate investor/speculators, with little regard for the level of suffering that results for the people of these countries in crisis, resulted in the continuity and intensification of institutional policies. This bleeding of the patient, likened to the use of leeches in the eighteenth century, weakens the body rather than restoring it to health. In Europe during the interwar years such insistence led to the rise of fascism. After the horrors of the Second World War, the United States changed course and offered the Marshall Plan to stimulate growth rather than insisting on more austerity, which would not only have unnecessarily prolonged Europe's pain but would in all likelihood have led to the election of communist governments and a fundamental change in the economic system of such major countries as France, Italy, and Germany.

A half-century later there was no Marshall Plan. When in 1998 Japan offered substantial aid to its East Asian neighbors to help them pursue expansionary policies rather than the harsh austerity prescription of the United States–dominated International Monetary Fund, the United States vetoed the plan (although as we shall see when we look at the episode of the East Asian financial crisis in the next chapter, Japan has pursued an independent involvement with the economies of the region). The United States insisted that the harsh conditionality imposed by the IMF was a necessary concomitant to financial help to those countries. Now that the Cold War was over and there was no longer any concern over the embrace of a communist alternative, the United States was able to play hardball with weaker economic formations, including would-be competitors. The U.S. insistence on market opening as the condition for new loans echoes their postwar demand that, as it became feasible in domestic terms, convertibility be established in Europe and for Japan, over the objections of the governments of these countries. In the 1960s and 1970s, despite strong resistance, especially by the French under General de Gaulle, and later Third World demands for a new international economic order, the United States was able to impose world financial and trade liberalization over all opposition. In the 1980s and 1990s it succeeded in achieving general global financial deregulation.

Indeed, the United States and the United Kingdom colluded to bring down the Bretton Woods regulatory framework. It was the initiative of these two nations that produced the Euromarkets and unleashed a process of competitive deregulation. The dismantling of capital controls was widely understood in Europe as designed to forestall the United States's relative economic and military decline. The United States forced countries to open financial markets or see capital leave their more regulated environments. Where strong controls prevented capital exiting, as in some emergent economies of the former Third World, the United States used the threat of exclusion from its markets.

The global institutions now set policy for a majority of the world's nations in the former communist countries and the Third World. The IMF lends money to debtor nations on strict conditionality that allows the fund to restructure their economies. The World Bank's structural adjustment programs involve similar guidance and encourage the same sort of subordination of domestic policies, especially those fostering protectionist measures and subsidies. Both operate within the terms of what is called the Washington Consensus, which insists on liberalization of markets, privatization of state enterprises, and other policies designed to encourage foreign investment, including devaluation and deregulation.

The fund and the bank have something of a good cop/bad cop relationship. The IMF imposes harsh conditionality on debtors. "IMF riots" have followed the announcement of agreements calling for the removal of government subsidies for food, transportation, and other basic needs of the poor in debtor countries and for the selling off of public assets to pay foreign banks and other creditors. The bank expresses concern at the suffering and the social costs of austerity measures. In recent years it has publicly criticized the IMF for poor judgment and for the harm done by its overly intrusive interference. The WB has extended a welcome to its critics, meeting with NGOs and asking their advice. It has backed away from some of the environmentally devastating mega-projects that have displaced indigenous populations and has focused on smaller-scale, locally initiated development (although it continues to fund ecologically disastrous energy extraction projects). Whether such changes and greater openness represent a fundamental change for WB or smart public relations tactics remains to be seen, but either way, the larger framing context of global state economic governance institutions remains. They are beholden to the resources provided by, and thus to the interests of, the economically powerful.

The WTO offers a forum through which countries can press the demands of their corporations. No nation has been more active than the United States in using the WTO to force open foreign markets and defend domestic industries. The organization has refused to entertain workers' rights and environmental protection as part of its charge and has used its power to force nations (including the United States) to abrogate other agreements and repeal national legislation (most famously legislation directed at protecting sea turtles from extinction) on the grounds that these "restrictions" were barriers to free trade. Such a stance has not endeared the WTO to environmentalists or labor rights activists.

The surrender of authority from national governments to global financial institutions was orchestrated by the leading economic powers, primarily the United States, which plays such a central role in shaping the new governance mechanisms and the ways they enforce policies congenial to U.S. economic interests. Weaker states have less choice and, of necessity, are in a more subservient role in these governance regimes. Transnational corporations and financial institutions are the major beneficiaries of the rules and enforcement mechanisms promulgated by the global financial institutions, although the policies they pursue are presented as representing the interests of all the world's citizens.

Resistance to the often-regressive distributional consequences of such policies has become vocal and organized. Increasingly, NGOs and popular mass movements have become significant players in the struggle to redefine economic and political rules appropriate to our era of globalization. Tension between these organizations of civil society and the instrumentalities of the dominant trilateral governments in North America, Europe, and Japan over the rules governing trade, investment, and finance have spilled into the streets since the Seattle protests of 1999.

Neoliberalism

The system of economic thought and practice that has taken the place of national Keynesianism is neoliberalism. As with national Keynesianism, it dominates both the economies of individual states and the global economy. Where national Keynesianism reflected the capacity of working people (in the United States and Europe) to resist the domination of corporate interests, neoliberalism can be seen as the imposition of the most powerful state—the United States—to overcome this resistance and impose its will on others.

The years since the end of the postwar era, perhaps since 1971 (when Richard Nixon, out of a desperation forged by American loss of competitiveness and an unwillingness to accept the domestic burdens of adjustment routinely imposed on others, unilaterally ended the Bretton Woods regime of fixed exchange rates) have been an extended period of attack on the presumptions, norms, and accommodations of the national Keynesian regulatory structures. This is because in an era of globalization the dominant forces in policy making are the most internationalized sectors of transnational corporations and financial institutions.

They are interested in penetrating local economies everywhere and oppose any restrictions to their freedom, including old-style regulation, which the national capitalists of each country once established to protect themselves from foreign competition. Increasingly, it became attractive to local capitalists to throw in their lot with these successful, globalized firms. The model based on national accumulation and protected domestic markets appeared no longer viable. A profound change in national state policies resulted. Nationalist laws and regulations were seen as unsuited to an era in which transnational capital was reconfiguring production and financial structures globally.

The opening of financial markets typically provokes speculative cycles of boom and bust. From the Mexican crisis evident in August 1982 through the Asian financial crises visible by 1997, problems with debt repayment increased the leverage of international capital and forced domestic restructuring on economies that had been attempting alternative development paths. Thus, the import substitution regimes in Latin America conceded local autonomy. Their elites embraced the globalist alternative insisted upon by creditors, the U.S. state apparatus, and the international financial institutions. In East Asia, state-led development regimes were forced to open their economies and foreign ownership increased. These countries had, through decades of successful development, forbidden foreign ownership in the financial and other key sectors of their economies. They were forced to open their economies on foreign terms. In Europe the Maastricht Treaty rules imposed austerity measures, reducing subsidies to state enterprises and encouraging their sale.

The United States has been remarkably successful in breaking the back of nationalist alternatives: in Latin America, the debt crisis of the 1980s was used to reorient local elites to insertion on a new basis of financial dependence; in the former communist world, the Soviet state was smashed and was replaced with the rule of neoliberal reformers; and in East Asia since 1997, state-led development regimes have been undermined. Financial crises have been used to gain leverage on these regimes, forcing them to deregulate and dispose of assets at distress prices. It is now time to repair some of the damage that was necessary to the desired restructuring.

These years of increased privatization of state enterprises, contracting out of government functions, and deregulation have been the negative moment, the process of destruction of the postwar regulatory order. By century's end there was growing concern that the cost in social unrest and system stability had become dangerously, and unnecessarily, high. The positive moment of the construction of a new financial architecture demanded by global capital provides equal treatment of corporations regardless of national origin in terms of investment freedom and equal standing before the law. In order to pressure governments who resist openness, international finance and trade organizations have been redesigned to enforce compliance with new rules of globality. The United States brought its own pressure with threats of retaliation, limiting access to its market, and cutting off financing. In the case of those "rogue" nations that opposed U.S. imperial design, there was military intervention, supposedly for humanitarian reasons. Whether this coercion involved the isolation of countries like Cuba or the bombing of nations such as Iraq and Serbia, whether such coercion and violence was unilateral by U.S. military forces, through NATO, or by UN resolution, as the only superpower, the United States exercised immense leverage.

Deregulating the Third World

Although national Keynesianism was most developed in the core capitalist countries—with relatively developed systems of welfare—a variant emerged in some regions of the periphery as well. The trade order preferred by the core countries for centuries was based on an international division of labor in which the periphery exported raw materials and imported manufactured goods. This regime had broken down during the Great Depression and the Second World War as trade patterns were disrupted. Out of necessity, Latin American countries had adopted import substitution industrialization, especially in the larger national economies. They could not import and so, making virtue of necessity, encouraged domestic industrialization. In the postwar period under the ideological leadership of the UN's Economic Commission for Latin America, led by the Argentinean economist Raul Prebisch, import substitution industrialization continued. Protectionist barriers were erected and subsidies were offered to domestic producers.

In this context, a Third World version of Keynesianism emerged that promoted production for the local market. The class alliance of the local development state was typically based on a historic bloc of industrialists and the urban masses under charismatic populist leadership with a powerful nationalist rhetoric. This nationalist-populist regime was essentially ended in Latin America by the debt crisis and the manner in which finance capital was able to force its resolution.

The construction of a new regulatory regime was facilitated by the demise of the Soviet Union. Previously, any country wishing an alternative development strategy to the one preferred by the United States could seek assistance from the Soviets. The Cold War competition encouraged the United States to exercise some constraint in its dealings with Third World countries. The struggle for the hearts and minds of the peoples of the Third World prompted foreign aid and, for "front line" states such as South Korea and Taiwan, the United States not only gave vast amounts of aid, but allowed statist economic development and preferential access to U.S. markets (as it had done for Japan when faced with the threat of a communist China since the 1950s). To prove that the American way of life was better than that of the communist, and to build strong economies on the borders of its enemies, the United States expended resources and allowed economic policies that it denied to others.

With the end of the Cold War it has been possible to shift political governance strategy in the Third World. During the Cold War years, the United States supported dictatorships, typically by military leaders capable of maintaining order, maintaining access to U.S. investors, and capable of dealing with "subversive" efforts to promote land reform, organize unions, and demand free and fair elections. The demise of the Soviet system coincided with a change in the economic relations between core and periphery of the world system. In the face of the destabilization and military options of the United States, the economic cost of countries to delink from the core countries, and without the option of support from the Soviets, the national liberation alternative became less viable.

By the 1980s and 1990s, given the overwhelming power of the United States on the one hand, and the lure of Western goods and especially advanced technologies, on the other, many of the military dictatorships that had been needed to prevent resistance to Western imperialism seemed anachronistic. These authoritarian governments, run by ruthless strongmen and incestuous familial elites, extorted rents from foreign and domestic businesses and maintained costly unproductive apparatuses of repression, which, when they were no longer vital, represented an unnecessary cost. In fact, by holding back the development of a market-oriented managerial class, they stood in the way of new-wave imperial designs. However, the sons of this ruling class ultimately became an active force in transforming the politics and economies of their countries. Elites in the periphery states have always sent their children abroad to be educated in the universities of the core. In the Reagan-Thatcher era they studied free market economics, received technical training, and returned to their countries to transform them along lines congenial to the rising tide of globalization. They embraced deregulation and privatization as part of their activity as an entrepreneurial class replacing direct governance by the military. They returned home to help restructure their economies along neoliberal lines. As a class, they also directly benefited from the transformation from statist to market dominated regimes. It was they who often arranged for, and then enriched themselves from, the privatization of state owned assets.

Part of the new paradigm of market opening was the increase in foreign borrowing. Both the bond market and, as these economies grew, local stock markets invited foreign finance. Investors were amply rewarded, encouraging further speculative inflow of capital. Local banks borrowed abroad at low rates and re-lent within the domestic market in local currencies, earning large profits on this carry trade. As foreign indebtedness grew and much of the money went to investments that proved unable over time to finance the repayment of borrowed funds, the speculative bubble broke. Capital flew out faster than it had flown in. Local currencies were depreciated, making it even more difficult to service debt denominated in foreign currencies, much of it on a floating-interest-rate basis. Debtors faced rising real repayment costs. To the extent that international financial institutions—regional development banks as well as the Bretton Woods institutions—responded by making new loans available to pay off foreign debt, the private investors were compensated. The countries themselves typically assumed the private sector's foreign debt. The growing debts were stretched out from short-term to long-term obligations, payable not only to the banks but also to agencies such as the International Monetary Fund, the World Bank, the InterAmerican Bank, and other multilateral lending agencies. The safeguard of such backup financing encouraged investors to lend in situations that, while not sustainable, offered opportunity for short-term profits and carried implicit guarantee against loss.

The international financial institutions functioned as lenders of last resort to prevent default. By extending new loans to pay off old ones, they drew these economies and their governments deeper into a set of relationships in which the agencies were able to dictate domestic economic policy measures that reoriented these countries even more toward neoliberal globalism. This is like an individual running over her credit line and finding that the credit card company was willing to raise her personal limit. Immediate default is prevented, but finance charges grow as payment is made over a longer period at high interest. Repayment is achieved with new loans. A larger and larger part of income goes into paying the interest on a growing debt. In the case of the very poorest countries, public lending agencies allowed some debt forgiveness. This permitted these heavily indebted countries to make larger payments to private lenders. The taxpayers of the rich countries subsidized international lenders and financial speculators indirectly by the forgiveness of publicly held debt extended to these governments by foreign aid agencies. Sometimes the private banks had to make concessions, but concessions within a context of long-term profitability from the loans. The foreign grip on the debtor economies tightened as a result of the way assistance was given in the crisis episodes.

The generalized overproduction, speculative excesses, and inflation of the 1970s thus led to basic restructuring pressures in both the core and the periphery. The defeat of working-class movements in the core as unions and left parties were hard pressed to offer an alternative theorization to the refrain of "there is no alternative" to restructuring austerity, and the demise of national liberation movements and populist alternatives in the periphery, often at the hands of United States–

trained death squads and militarist terror, contributed to a class recomposition in both the core and periphery countries and ultimately to a change in consciousness. The professional and technical strata came to see its interests tied to the further expansion and success of transnational capital.

Restructuring in the Core

In the core, those whose incomes allowed for investment in 301(k) plans and other investment vehicles saw the growth in stock market valuations as a source of substantial wealth. As financial portfolios fattened, luxury consumption grew—the result of what economists call the wealth effect. Most Americans, however, did not own stock either directly or through pension plans or other indirect forms of ownership. Many have borrowed more deeply to sustain living standards in the face of stagnant real income. While productivity grew, working-class income did not. The profit share increased, producing a widening gap between returns from financial investment and return to labor time.

The mergers and acquisitions of the 1980s and 1990s, the leveraged buyouts funded with "junk bonds," and the downsizing and restructuring that followed the deindustrialization era in the 1970s as older basic industries rationalized production through massive layoffs and plant closings, were complemented by the white-collar layoffs of the 1980s and 1990s, which affected office workers and middle management as well as blue-collar workers. The United States led the world in the reorganization of its economy, setting a pattern that was adopted to a lesser extent by Europeans and Japanese capital. What had been interpreted as a loss of competitiveness had in fact produced dramatic downsizing that left U.S. capital in a stronger position, even as the working class paid the high price of the adjustment to restore profitability. The profit squeeze experienced by U.S. corporations in the 1970s eased as a result of this massive restructuring and redistribution, a result of the austerity imposed on the working class whose real wages stopped rising after 1973. Unit labor costs fell (or rose more slowly) in the United States; real wage growth lagged Europe and Japan, to the benefit of U.S. capital.

In the United States the unemployment rate fell with the growth of lower-wage, part-time, and generally more "flexible" patterns of employment. As unemployment rose in Europe, capital negotiated a single currency for an expanded Common Market. The idea was that corporations in Europe, able to sell without restrictions on a continent-wide basis, would enjoy economies of scale. Greater competition would lower cost. A single currency would make costs transparent and put further pressure on wages and prices. The more efficient firms would grow as a single market for Europe became a reality. As this occurred workers and governments would compete for footloose industry.

The adoption of a single currency required a closer harmonization of fiscal policies and control by a European central bank. This meant loss of national independence in monetary policy. The member countries adopted a common set of criteria for joining the single-currency zone. These measures called for limits on public debt and national rates of inflation. Thus, they imposed austerity on European countries, which tightened their macro policies even at the cost of a massive rise in unemployment. It was the Maastricht Treaty–mandated macroeconomic policies in Europe that produced the extremely high levels of unemployment, pain deemed necessary for future growth in a pattern reminiscent of the austerity that Third World debtors had been forced to undergo at the behest of the IMF and other international lenders. Competition for jobs clipped the wings of trade unions. Capital also forced tax concessions from governments.

Is There an Alternative?

Jeffrey Sachs, the Harvard economist and "debt doctor," has criticized the IMF, "loyal to financial orthodoxy and mindful of creditors to the neglect of debtor countries," for often pouring oil on the flames instead of putting out the financial fires.[1] But there is method to the seeming ineptitude. By making matters harder for the debtors, the IMF maximizes its own leverage in forcing changes on these governments that would not otherwise be made. The policies that it insists upon transform local economies and government practices to the advantage of foreign capital. While this critique will be explored at length, the more immediately influential criticism of the IMF comes from the free-market political right who believe that the IMF creates moral hazard problems by guaranteeing insurance against investor loss, thus encouraging speculators to take greater risks than they otherwise would, which ultimately produces the very consequences that the IMF, in theory, is dedicated to minimizing. Right-wing nationalists object to the one-world government aspect of these international agencies, which they see as undermining U.S. sovereignty and placing a burden on U.S. taxpayers. Free market economists who oppose the role of the international financial institutions believe that markets can discipline investors and governments by rewarding sound practices and punishing irresponsible ones.

But this argument fails to engage the centuries-long experience of speculative excesses and debt cycles that preceded the formation of the International Monetary Fund in 1944. These critics come closer to the heart of the matter when they denounce the U.S. executive branch of government that, under the guidance of the leading elements of finance capital, has been the architect of these policies and institutions. Right-wing populism captures something of the reality of elite domination, but lacking a class analysis tends to blame these developments on social planners, the Jews, or other supposedly conspiratorial groups, rather than rooting their critique in an examination of a basic understanding of capitalism. They tend to celebrate competitive, individualistic free markets and do not theorize about the historical process through which monopoly capital and the reign of finance has been created. They seek to move us back to a mythic free market, rather than forward to a system that is capable of socializing capital in the general interest. The blind spot of the radical right is to think that these international agencies (to say nothing of the black helicopters) are the tools of some shadowy world government UN conspiracy rather than their own state and treasury departments. By separating government (bad) from free enterprise (good) they fail to see the interpenetration of U.S.-based transnational capital and the emergent international state apparatuses. By idealizing competition and demonizing the state they misrepresent both the political nature of the economy and the class nature of the state.

Liberal institutionalists back the role of the IMF, if not its every action. They stress the need for surveillance by technocrats able to oversee the gathering of accurate and timely information so that market participants can make informed decisions and thus contribute to the prevention of panic when the extent of a crisis situation is unexpectedly and suddenly disclosed. Once panic sets in, it is every investor for him or herself, and more rational solutions, from a social standpoint, are made difficult if not impossible due to the problem of overcoming collective action problems. New loans and loan guarantees from international financial institutions can calm markets and allow more rational solutions, it is said. Once investors know the money will be there they feel less need to pull out. Liberal institutionalists portray the international financial institutions as run by technicians who are for the most part nonpolitical in their actions, acting to encourage better practices by investors and governments alike. By encouraging creditors to act collectively in support of mutually beneficial workout programs, international agencies can limit the cost of resolving financial panics, liberal institutionalists argue. This would give the countries involved the breathing room to deal with their problems.

Critics on the left suggest that international financial institutions are managed in the context of the power and prerogatives of transnational finance capital. For those who stand outside and are critical of the ideologies generated by the powerful, these agencies can be seen as wielding access to loans and the conditions that go with them as weapons of financial terrorism. Just as bombings and the calculated threat of the use of violence against Third World countries were characteristic of the age of gunboat diplomacy, so denial of monetary credit is capable of turning oil tankers around mid-ocean and denying food shipments to hungry people whose governments do not cooperate with the financial diplomacy of international financial institutions.

Critics on the left believe that international financial institutions are enforcers for finance capital in precisely the same way that U.S. marines were enforcers in an earlier age. Of course the marines and other branches of the armed forces are not at all absent from the present world scene where military interventions continue to play an important role. The cost to U.S. taxpayers of such "bailouts" is believed to be less important than the support that international financial institutions give to the dominance of finance capital to control the lives of people around the world. At a deeper level, orthodoxy's claim that deregulated financial markets produce "correct" pricing of capital assets is viewed as an ideological assertion reinforced in the mainstream propaganda so effectively that for many people it is difficult to believe that the IMF solution, and neoliberalism more broadly, is not scientific, or that there is any alternative to the logic of the pure market, as if something like a pure market could be approximated in a world structured by fundamentally unequal power relations.

But it is only possible to offer alternatives to neoliberalism once we have understood the interests that it embodies and advances. One reason for the unseemly haste to enforce new financial rules and to enshrine the freedom of capital from political interference is that a vast amount of learning has gone on; citizens throughout the world are increasingly aware of the effect of growing concentration and social unaccountability of finance capital and transnational corporations. The efficiency argument for financial globalization ignores distributional costs and the possible systemic disruption unregulated capital flows can cause. It also denies the priority for equitable and socially just economic policies in the larger context of the goals an inclusive democratic society sets for itself. Once the neoliberal logic is accepted, a variety of social regulations become problematic, from minimum wages to the rights of workers to organize and bargain collectively with employers. Social regulations can be redefined as impediments to flexible labor markets.

International financial institutions have forced a reduction of government programs in countries around the world. Arthur MacEwan, commenting on the enforcement of anti-working-class policies in the name of efficiency, has written: "Considering the logic of the World Bank and IMF policy makers, one wonders how long it will be until they require countries receiving their largesse to abolish laws against slavery." [2] Either social welfare is rolled back or the privileges of capital need to be restricted. Social control of capital is necessary for the greater freedom and well-being of working people who are otherwise forced to make continued sacrifices to capital. Without social regulation, rules that limit the mobility and "freedom" more generally of capital, other rules are adopted, ones that take away hard-won victories of working people.

It is possible to envision effective capital controls. The argument that banks and hedge funds would simply go offshore to jurisdictions where regulation is minimal is not a strong one. Certainly, if the United States were to announce that it would not accept monetary transfers into its domestic banking system from banks and other financial institutions located in jurisdictions that do not regulate capital flows in strict fashion, these havens would quickly conform or else footloose capital would soon move to zones from which they would have access to U.S. markets. If the United States were to adopt such procedures, other nations would quickly fall in line. It is the political barrier to meaningful regulation, the power of finance capital in the councils of the American state, that is the issue and not some natural economic law.

I expect greater controls will be put in place for the good of finance capital; regulation can be envisioned that will smooth the way for more secure accumulation, such as standstill provisions in loans that will force creditors from pulling capital out individually until a negotiated recovery plan is in place. Such reforms would moderate panics and limit damages caused by uncontrolled capital flight. Changes in bankruptcy laws might be suggested, and so on. It is the unwillingness of capital to submit, its strength, and the power of political allies that have prevented even reforms that are in its own interest from being adopted—until painful lessons have been learned. As in earlier periods of regulation, when the Federal Reserve, the Securities and Exchange Commission, and a host of other regulatory instruments were adopted, capital will object that such proposals are unworkable, socialist in origin, dangerous, and un-American. After reforms that adopted, they will prove to strengthen the power of the elites and not weaken them. More radical reform will be staved off unless there is massive popular pressure. The development of such a militant movement from below will need to be accompanied by a reinterpretation of globalization as a phenomenon best described as twenty-first-century imperialism.

The Higher Risk Society and the Welfare State

While the basic rules have not changed, globalization and the neo-liberal policy climate have led analysts to observe that we are living with "a combination of growth and uncertainty that they have never seen before" (the "never" might apply to the life experience of some of those who came to maturity during the era of national Keynesianism in positions of relative privilege). The combination has been familiar to working people throughout history. The epochal shift from national Keynesianism to neoliberal globalism can be seen in terms of increasing uncertainty. As Michael Mandel, an analyst of contemporary economic developments and *Business Week* editor, writes: "Welcome to the high-risk society. It's not the society our parents grew up with, stable and secure. Instead, this economy is becoming much more like the financial markets. Consider: Ordinary investors in the financial markets would love safety—but they are driven to higher-risk investments such as stock, which offer better long-term returns. Now, this same risk-return trade-off pervades the whole economy. Individuals and companies would like to run from uncertainty. But they cannot." [3]

High-risk finance, in which speculators make huge profits but accept high risks, has a counterpart in the real economy when workers who can take advantage of a window of opportunity by developing the skills needed for high-demand jobs may be well rewarded. But, as Mandel has noticed, the analogy between financial markets and the real economy is not perfect. "Money can be switched between stocks in moments. By contrast, it may take years to renovate a factory or learn a new skill." [4] And even if we act more quickly these days many are left behind and left out. Workers are not compensated for the years they have put in or given the wherewithall to either retire without a vast decrease in living standard. Nor is it realistic to think most can recycle themselves to be software engineers and communications entrepreneurs of some hot new startup. Older-generation displaced workers are simply thrown away in the age-old pattern of capitalist redistributive growth. Some are at higher risk in the high-risk society than others.

The analogy to financial markets is flawed in another respect as well. Financial speculators whose bets go wrong in Third World countries find that IMF loans provide them with a bailout. So as not to lose the confidence of markets, monies are recycled back to the core countries as payment for speculative investments that had been at risk, saved by the public monies of the international institutional lenders.

Clearly, the high-risk society has undermined social solidarities and hurt working people. One result of this that deserves special mention, because it is a ticking time bomb, is the end of the company pension. As companies cut costs by cutting pension benefits, individual savings for the majority do not make up the need for retirement. Actuaries use as a rule of thumb the idea that people need nine times final salary to buy an annuity of about two-thirds final salary. But most workers cannot come near this on their own. In the past, as one pension expert says, "we've had the family, the state, and the employer. But soon it'll be only the cold flush of capitalism." [5]

Individual working people and ordinary citizens cannot escape the constraints and coercive freedom of the high-risk society. Collective action to control excessive risk taking, the establishment of protective legislation and rules for investment, which internalize social cost, offer some protection from the destabilizing forces of the unregulated market and the norms of neoliberal capitalist social relations. In a society that gives unbridled freedom to the power of Schumpeterian growth and in which the gales of creative destruction revolutionize the means of production, the securities of an age can be swept aside, as this generation is not alone in having experienced. Writers in the financial press accept the high-risk casino society as inevitable and good for us. They discount the fate of its many victims.

The Political Face of Globalization

In an era of no growth in working-class income, lower taxation has wide appeal. It becomes a sound electoral strategy to promise "no new taxes." This is not only the promise of conservative parties but of the reborn left-of-center parties best exemplified by "new Labour" in England. On taking power in the late 1990s, the New Labour party introduced an austerity budget more stringent than that the Tories had insisted upon. Tony Blair, something of a Clinton clone, not only promised no increase in income taxes during the first Labor administration in decades, but made welfare reform a key objective of his government. His "third way," a triangulation strategy not unlike Clinton's, distances him from the traditional working-class base of his party and the welfare society it had promoted. After decades of conservative rule, it was widely said that the welfare state is electorally unsustainable. By that, it is meant that voters won't pay for an effective public sector committed to individual dignity, inclusiveness, and egalitarian values. They may want services but they prefer lower taxes. This line of thinking goes: "We" believe we can better spend our money than government bureaucrats can. The class nature of such a formulation should not go unnoticed. For those who are wealthy enough to afford better quality services in the market, paying taxes for provision of these services is a fool's choice. If the rich and the poor pool their money, the average level of the service provided is bound to be a major improvement for the poor but a step or three down for the rich. The better-off prefer to provide for themselves on the market and not be subjected to the level of public service provision that the masses must accept because they cannot afford anything else.

The greater the proportion of the citizenry that relies on public provision, the better the service is likely to be because more of the better-off will involve themselves in working to improve the quality of what they as well as others receive. Once public services are only for the poor they are far more likely to be poor quality services. This can be seen in a country like Sweden in which the tax burden is 60 percent or so of average income and yet people want to spend more, not less, on welfare. This seems surprising, but as the *Economist* writes in an article detailing the victory of the Social Democrats in 1998, "most taxpayers are also welfare recipients, and are happy to cough up for good child-care centers and lavish pensions."[6]

National capitalisms in most European countries have, as in Sweden, enjoyed a close corporate-government cooperation that involved something of a class compromise. The welfare state was popular with voters represented by social democratic, socialist, communist and labor parties of various complexions. State power was used to encourage the growth of national firms with a host of incentives and subsidies and by protecting domestic markets from foreign competition. Deals were done within relatively small circles.

The problem that developed is that national champions, state-owned or private, have not easily adjusted to globalization. Indeed the very basis of their existence, the presumption of a viable national scale economy with controlled international trade, has eroded. In the new world economy, transnational takeovers and mergers become inevitable despite efforts to gain competitiveness through industrial policy and consolidation on a national basis. The hemorrhaging of state budgets from subsidies to increasingly less competitive national champions has also driven privatization, even if some governments have vetted the choice of shareholders and takeover partners. The sheltered national environments have cracked. The demands of globalized capitalists have been harder to resist and their demands have also driven the privatization trend. Capital moves abroad when it can to avoid the taxation that is the basis of the welfare state.

With the globalization by the leading segments of capital they have less allegiance to a particular place. As they become more footloose the fate of any particular community becomes less important for them. The nation is less a community of which they are a part. It becomes only one market area among many. Under a regime of national Keynesianism, the purchasing power of the nation's consumers is crucial. They are the market. In an era of global neoliberalism, taxation and labor costs at "home" must compete with foreign locations. Markets more than in the past are planet-wide and so is competition. The workers of the home country lose whatever relatively privileged treatment they once enjoyed unless they are organized and capable of a politically effective presence and are willing to regulate capital. Redistributional state policies, always a burden to the extent that capital is taxed for its provision, becomes an unnecessary cost in the eyes of transnational capital. More routinely, an electoral coalition from the top replaces the broader and more inclusive coalition of the postwar national Keynesian regime.

If the welfare state implied egalitarianism and citizen entitlements, the high-risk society is about self-help and personal responsibility, the transfer of the state's role to private insurers, mutual aid, and charity. And while conservative politicians raised these alternatives first, it has been the third way corporate liberals who have been more successful in dismantling the welfare state and undermining its broad ideological support. The emphasis on society over state stressed by Thatcher and Reagan, who saw government as the problem and not the solution, has its kinder, gentler, and more effective formulation under Clinton and Blair. Was this trip necessary?

It is often said that the success of American-style capitalism has been so dramatic that Europe, Japan, and the rest of the world has no choice but to adapt to the one and only best model of capitalism. But if we look at the actual performance of these economies over the last thirty or forty years it has been much stronger than the Anglo-American model. Over the shorter period since the second half of the 1990s, real GNP growth slowed but still increased as much over the decade in the European Union and Japan as in the United States. Taking the longer view, capital stock increased more, as did the productivity of capital employed per worker, and real wages grew faster in these economies than in the United States. Significantly, profits did not. It is also true that in the 1990s there was higher unemployment in Europe and increasingly in Japan (where much of it takes the form of hidden employment as Japanese firms keep on unneeded employees rather than simply firing them as would happen in America), yet average wages were higher in Japan, Germany, and other Western European nations. In these countries the unemployed are treated far better than in the United States in terms of benefits. The distribution of economic growth matters. If we take Bill Gates's income, yours, and mine, and divide by three, statistically you and I will be far richer. The statistical illusion of average income obscures rising inequalities. "Average" income or the increase in productivity of the average worker in an economy are not better measures if the distribution of benefits is such that the majority of the people do not receive any of the increase. This was the case in the United States. For working people, averages did not begin to measure standard of living differences since inequality in the United States was so much greater than elsewhere in the advanced capitalist world.

What makes describing the economy so difficult is that almost all the material that shapes our consciousness comes from a media fixated on the rate of return to investors. It is not simply that even a five-minute news summary must include a stock market report. It is that coverage, especially of foreign events, is so much in terms of how developments affect investors. Thus the Russian or Mexican economies are discussed in terms of debt owed to foreigners and the ability to repay. Once expectations firm up, the country drops from the news until there is a change that will affect the value of investors' holdings. That the people of the country may be suffering over a prolonged period, or an economy functions badly, is not of interest if markets have expected these events. It merits mention only in an ideological context that blames problems on the legacy of statist practices and institutions. Only a change in market expectations is important for investors. Media coverage is geared to their need to know and not to informing people on broader socio-economic circumstances. Political events are judged important primarily in terms of how they may impact on conditions that affect investors. The poor, and the majority of the people who are the working class, are uninteresting except to the extent their activity changes, or threatens to change, the profit picture. The information economy is thus a purveyor of a class perspective and to this extent often an agency of disinformation. It is capital that is dynamic. Workers are inert, acted upon, and not the actors in this telling. It is just such an understanding of social relations, of politics, and of agency that the emergent twenty-first-century movement of social justice seeks to challenge.

CHAPTER FOUR

Globalization as the Imperialism of Finance

The Vocabulary of Imperialism

It is illuminating to consider the global economy at the start of the twenty-first century in terms of the framework of imperialism. We may think of WTO rules and IMF and World Bank conditionality and structural adjustment loans as representing the "Internationale" of capital, which, like the imperialism of free trade evident a century ago, takes it as a duty to coerce territories incapable of achieving free trade on their own into modernizing economic practices for their own good. This was true also of the expansion of the formal British Empire in the second half of the nineteenth century, when moderate free traders believed that "civilized" powers should impose appropriate institutions in those parts of the world where the local institutional framework was not conducive to peaceful and open trade. If the triumph of Great Britain's insistence on free trade and America's "Open Door" demands were strategies to expand empire by a different name, and on the cheap, the global state economic governance institutions are the heirs to a longer tradition.

At the end of the twentieth century, as Jeffrey Sachs tells us, for perhaps half of the developing world outside of China and India,

> the IMF is an all-too-constant presence, almost a surrogate government in financial matters. Not unlike the days when the British Empire placed senior

officials directly into the Egyptian and Ottoman ministries, the IMF is insinuated into the inner sanctums of nearly seventy-five developing-country governments around the world—countries with a combined population of some 1.4 billion. These governments rarely move without consulting the IMF staff, and when they do, they risk their lifelines to capital markets, foreign aid, and international respectability. Newspaper headlines in these countries herald the comings and goings of IMF staff. [1]

It is not difficult to see such intrusion within the frame of imperialism. In order to do this, however, it is necessary to recognize both the differences between the global context of today and the classical period of imperialism as territorial acquisition and direct subjection of distant societies to the power of an imperialist state. Imperialism is not simply about territorial acquisition, but more broadly involves gaining political and economic control over other peoples and lands, whether by military force or more subtle means. It is a matter of state policy and practice extending power and domination, often by economic means.

This was recognized by the classical theorists of imperialism from J. A. Hobson through V. I. Lenin and Rosa Luxemburg to Nikolai Bukharin. What these early theorists of imperialism had in common was an appreciation of the nature of capitalism as a world system in which the core economies exerted power over the periphery, competed with each other for influence and control, and jockeyed for position, using whatever means they had at their disposal to favor the leading factions of their own capitalist class in a globalist competition with the capitals of other state formations. Whether speaking of "the white man's burden," "the civilizing mission," "stopping communist aggression," "making the world safe for democracy," "the Monroe Doctrine," "the Truman Doctrine," or "stopping genocide," the rationales have always been secondary to the goal of commanding the resources of other nations. The exploitation of the domestic working class, while it implies the use of class power, can be one of seemingly free exchange. In the case of the relation of the hegemonic powers to the weaker nations, military conquest and threats of economic coercion and force to obtain de facto domination of other governments and territories has been the *modus vivendi* of imperialism.

Although imperialism has had a moral overtone—at least since the time of Lenin—of unjustifiable exploitation of some nations by the

leading capitalists of others who use state power to achieve their dominance, this moral dimension was not central to the analyses. The
originators of the construct, notably John Hobson, saw a justification
for financial invasion and market dominance in the necessity of core
capital to expand to the more underdeveloped parts of the world to
avoid domestic crisis. They defended the right of more civilized peoples
to impose progress upon lower cultures. In Germany Karl Kautsky, the
leading theorist of the Second International, argued that colonies were
a prerequisite for capitalist expansion and an important factor in the
then supremacy of Great Britain. Outside markets were crucial for
national capitalist development. Kautsky saw the emergence of international cartels as the precursor to cooperation among national capitals.
He perceived an international homogenization at work that would
inhibit national rivalries. He foresaw a merging of national capitals into
a single global ruling class. This, he believed, would produce peaceful
movement toward ultra-imperialism. Kautsky himself proposed a non-
militaristic European federation, a sort of European Union.

These early theorists of imperialism emphasized its role in creating
a single, interconnected global economy. Leon Trotsky was among those
who recognized that the world economy was not the simple addition of
its natural units, but a powerful independent reality created by the
international division of labor and by the world market that dominates
all national markets. But this did not dampen his optimism about the
modernizing potential of capital's penetration of noncapitalist regions
along the lines of much of Marx's own writings on colonialism. In this,
his view was similar to Bukharin's, who conceptualized "a system of
production relations and, correspondingly, of exchange relations on a
world scale." [2] Bukharin wrote of the thickening network of international economic relations in which capitalist forces of production were
inseparable from the internationalization of the division of labor.
"[T]here grows an extremely flexible economic structure of world
capitalism, all parts of which are mutually interdependent," he wrote.
"The slightest change in one part is immediately reflected in all." [3]

Such discussions were not confined to Marxist circles. Their themes
were echoed by such theorists as Hobson and University of Wisconsin
political science professor Paul Samuel Reinsch, who was not only

influential among academics but also advised the U.S. Departments of State and War. Reinsch distinguished between the older settler imperialism, which left the host society relatively untouched, and modern capitalist-investment imperialism, which "in contrast, went to the very heart of the host societies' internal affairs at the outset, transforming basic class relations, social structures, and political institutions. Hence, it brought with it colossal and rapid upheavals in the host lands and in world politics, unprecedented in human history." [4]

Just as Kautsky saw ultra-imperialism, the emergence of a globalized ruling class, as an unproblematic development, and failed to note the tensions and rivalries that produced conflicts among and between capitals, so today those who describe globalization in similar terms underestimate the importance of inter-imperialist rivalry, and, more broadly, intra-ruling-class divisions, and typically exhibit a historical amnesia with regard to the innate instability of capitalism. The narrative of capitalism's triumph does not include overinvestment and resultant excess capacity, intense competition for markets, deflationary trends, or crises. If we are to understand globalization in our time and the politics that surround it and develop a program for social and economic justice, it is useful, indeed necessary, to take a longer view.

In each period the contradictions among national capitals have sparked costly conflict. While a hundred years ago it was "the scramble for Africa" that presaged the violent eruption of inter-imperialist rivalries that became the First World War, in the present period globalization inspires IMF conditionality with its devastating impacts and trade wars. It is true, however, that globalization has developed to the point where interpenetration through direct foreign and portfolio investments and the growth of strategic alliances, subcontracting, and commodity chain patterns of production moderate conflict among the core powers. In addition, the dominant position of the United States enforces an order that was absent a century ago with the decline of unquestioned British hegemony.

The Modern Imperialism of Finance

The continuities between territorial imperialism and contemporary globalization can be located historically by returning to the conditions that brought an end to the postwar period of national Keynesianism. This can be dated from 1971, the year that Nixon unilaterally ended the Bretton Woods system, or from 1973, when world leaders agreed to accept a floating exchange rate system in place of the fixed exchange rate regime, or from 1974, when the United States abolished all restrictions on international capital movements. It could also be dated from 1989—the end of Soviet communism, the fall of the Berlin Wall, and the reunification of Germany. Future historians might move the end of the postwar era into the 1990s when France and Italy, in 1990, and Spain and Portugal, in 1992, abolished capital controls. To some extent the choice of date is arbitrary—the point is that in these years something we associate with globalization became evident and something we call the postwar era dominated by the national Keynesian welfare state came to an end, and the world entered a period dominated by global neoliberalism and the imperialism of finance. We have discussed this transition as it affected the scope and character of state power and changed the role of global financial institutions such as the IMF. In this chapter, the transformation is approached by focusing on the liberation of financial markets.

In this sphere too, the global economy has been transformed in the decades since about 1970. In the early 1970s daily foreign exchange trading amounted to $10 billion to $20 billion. By 2000, daily foreign exchange trading was $1.6 trillion or seventy-five times world trade. Currency exchanges that had been theorized as primarily tied to demand for goods and services had overwhelmingly come to be dominated by short-term speculative purposes. Moreover, rather than stimulating more rapid economic growth and increased real investment, these dramatic monetary flows were accompanied by a disturbingly slow growth rate of the world economy. Slow growth was ironically the preferred pattern of investors who feared lowered returns from rising inflation. Slower growth was a conscious policy choice for many governments trying to protect their currencies from appreciation and resultant price pressures and loss of international competitiveness.

Europe provides one prominent example of this pattern. During the 1980s, countries joining the European exchange rate mechanism (ERM) were forced to keep domestic interest rates high to prevent exchange rates from declining in violation of the ERM target range. This slowed growth and increased both unemployment and government deficits. In a famous episode in 1982, George Soros is said to have made a billion dollars over the weekend betting that Britain would be unable to defend the value of the pound. The long-term high unemployment and slow growth in Europe are in significant measure the result of first the ERM of the 1980s and, in the 1990s, of Maastricht Treaty requirements for those wishing to join the single European currency, which called for austerity and deflationary policies, which weakened the working class and strengthened the hand of capital, especially transnational capital, and dramatically raised unemployment rates in Europe.

Under the new regime of neoliberalism, any economy trying to stimulate growth through fiscal stimulus will see their imports and rate of inflation increase, the value of their currency fall. Their only protection from these developments in an internationally liberalized financial market is to keep interest rates high. This slows economic growth. Deregulation of financial markets increases deflationary pressures, as nations wishing to attract foreign capital must keep their interest rates up even if this has deflationary impacts on their economies. Financial deregulation has produced the highest real interest rates in modern times, not the promised lower interest rates that competitive market theory would suggest. Floating exchange rates have intensified competition and diminished the capacities of individual states to control capital and to tax it effectively. These developments have weakened the progressive movements and have moved governments to the right politically. They have dramatically increased the profits of the largest global corporations in a pattern we have described as redistributive growth: from workers to capital, and especially the most international sectors of capital, and from the peripheries to the core, especially to the United States.

Even those countries that have been able to attract a significant flow of foreign capital have found it to be short-term and volatile. Inflows produce domestic inflation, growing imports, balance of trade problems, and then the collapse of the value of the domestic currency and capital flight as the real rate of growth in interest rates exceeds the rate of growth in GDP. This leads debt burdens to become unsustainable.

This pattern, which has created fiscal crisis for Latin America in the 1980s and for East Asia, as well as the continued slow growth and high unemployment in Europe, is created by the unregulated capital flows of the post–Bretton Woods era. It has been accelerated by the insistence of the world's central bankers and global economic institutions, acting on behalf of international finance capital, that states unilaterally disarm and remove restrictions on foreign penetration. Most importantly, it has been the United States executive branch and especially the Clinton administration's Treasury Department that have insisted on the economic policies that devastated so many countries around the world.

In interpreting the policies of finance capital many observers, both mainstream analysts and some on the left, have seen the destructive impact of neoliberalism's financial demands as suggesting a "paradox." Crotty, Epstein, and Kelly, for example, write:

> Studies overwhelmingly indicate that foreign direct investment is attracted by high levels of demand, high quality infrastructure, and high levels of skills and human capital. . . . [They cite academic sources for this view.] Yet the process of foreign direct investment and capital mobility within the neo-liberal structure undermines those very factors that attract and sustain MNCs [multinational corporations]. Short-term capital mobility and austerity undermine demand; and destructive tax competition and low demand undermine government and private investment in infrastructure and human capital. . . . In the neo-liberal regime, countries find it increasingly difficult to offer companies what they need; and in the long run, companies may find it increasingly difficult to get the demand, infrastructure, and skills that they want. [5]

Of course, this paradox is of long standing. As dependency theorists long ago demonstrated, there is a pattern of imperialist penetration that takes advantage of local resources, with no interest in the sustained growth of local economies, and then leaves them for greener fields elsewhere when profit considerations dictate. The idea that industrial export platform economies were different from primary extraction economies rests on the now discredited view that dependent development through export-oriented industrialization represents a qualitatively different pattern of growth. Transnational corporations move to higher profit venues more easily as national barriers to capital flow and internationally enforced agreements supporting the "right" to free entry and easy exit minimize the costs of moving on when once desirable local circumstances have been degraded. Under such conditions, the state loses whatever moral authority it possessed as the holders of real power have by then moved their wealth offshore. The number of failed states in the world, and the deteriorated conditions of others, who despite following IMF-sanctioned polices have not found their economies growing, attest to the limits of the model. The unrelenting attack on the state may well create a more laissez-faire economy, but such a regulatory regime erodes its capacities to provide adequate conditions for growth over an extended time. Governments have become less able to fund quality education and physical infrastructure to complement private sector accumulation.

We have seen how much harm financial collapse leaves in its wake. It takes a long time for excess capacity and global gluts to be worked off. In the globalization process of the last decades of the twentieth century, financial capital used the power of the American state to profit from the adversity of others. That elected officials were generally more concerned with accommodating financiers, allowing them to reconstruct global regulatory institutions, sends the rest of us a clear message as to who is expendable in the new world order. It is not the weakness of the state that is revealed in these developments but the class character of the capitalist state. The applicability of the imperialist frame contrasts with the mainstream treatment of these developments. This is most obvious as we consider further the emergent international financial regime.

The International Monetary Fund as a Tool of Imperialism

While the mainstream critiques of the IMF's transformative strategy have become most pervasive among academics and other intellectuals and policy analysts it has been generally framed in terms of "paradoxes" and "mistakes." In this regard, it is certainly true that the IMF's harsh austerity conditionality is "horrifying," as Martin Wolf, the *Financial Times* columnist, writes, "For what the IMF is saying (to acclaim from market participants, central banks, and ministries of finance around the world) is that the only way for a government to restore market confidence is to demonstrate its willingness to inflict social misery on itself and its society. This is, in short, a masochist's route to credibility." [6]

There is, however, method in the masochism. It is the asymmetry in the treatment of the lenders and borrowers, the haves and the have-nots, that has been systematic. The lenders expect, and get, favorable treatment. This, as has been widely pointed out, creates what economists call the moral hazard problem: it is attractive to engage in international lending, even at considerable risk. Investors given this insurance are more likely to make unsound investments because someone will bail them out. The asymmetry, a result of the structural power imbalance between lenders and borrowers, imposes severe austerity on the people of the borrowing country in order to help the lenders to come out on top. The IMF insists debtor countries adopt high interest rates to protect their currencies and so restore investor confidence. The rationale is that if interest rates are high enough to more than compensate for expected depreciation of the country's currency, investors will expect a high return on their money; therefore capital flight and its harmful effects on the economy will be avoided. But until investors come to believe the local economy and the currency have bottomed out, this rate must be exceedingly high to prevent currency flight. Such rates increase domestic bankruptcies, as local firms are unable to borrow for necessary business functions. This produces unemployment and the misery of the masses. High interest rates also place extreme burdens on governments. The cost of financing national debt rises dramatically, pushing government budgets deep into deficit, and sparking IMF demands that more austerity measures be taken. Hence the "masochist" solution is painful but hardly successful from the perspective of those forced to endure such policies. The costly "mistakes" are felt by those directly impacted. The solutions imposed by the U.S. Treasury and the IMF are not mistakes from the perspective of the banks and the bondholders.

One important aspect of the redistributive design of such policies is to force the weaker governments to accept as their own burden debts owed by the private sector of their countries (by companies unable to pay), which the international financiers demand be repaid, although these governments had not borrowed the money or even guaranteed the debt. As financial observers recognized in the case of the East Asian fast growing economies in 1997 and 1998, and in the case of Brazil a year or so later,

these were countries that did not have particularly high public indebtedness. As Wolf writes of the situation of Brazil:

> Brazil's public indebtedness is not particularly high. Moreover, the country has
> a primary fiscal surplus (balance, without interest payments), targeted at 3.1
> percent of GDP for this year. Thus Brazil's fiscal deficit of 8 percent of GDP last
> year is entirely explained by interest payments. Its difficulty, however is that the cost
> of 70 percent of its domestic debt is determined at the floating exchange rate. . . . So
> high interest rates are themselves the chief cause of the loss of confidence in domestic
> monetary stability that they are expected to cure. Worse, if the impact of high interest
> rates on the economy is bad enough, even the primary budget surplus is likely to
> disappear, as revenues contract and spending on goods and services rises. This then
> is a true vicious circle. Brazil is trying to restore confidence with policies that seem
> bound first to undermine it. [7]

The Brazilian problems, the East Asian financial crisis, European slow
growth, the horrendous situation in Russia, and so on, are all part of the
larger story of the imperialism of finance, which forces the nations of
the world to transform their economies to accommodate its demands.
In each instance the threat and practice of capital flight has been the
battering ram forcing down the walls national economies had erected
against foreign control. In each instance local elites attracted by the
benefits of foreign loans, technology, and markets had attempted to
negotiate a relation to the world economy that offered better terms for
local capital only to be rebuked by transnational capital, which, taking
advantage of the crises of overextension that are a natural part of
capitalist accumulation, demanded market openings. As Martin Khor,
director of the Third World Network in Malaysia has described it,
structural adjustment is "a policy to continue colonial trade and economic patterns developed during the colonial period, but which the
Northern powers want to continue into the post-colonial period. Economically speaking, we are more dependent on the ex-colonial countries than we ever were. The World Bank and IMF are playing the role
that our ex-colonial masters used to play."

The debt crises in the 1980s and 1990s allowed the IMF and World
Bank to impose the Washington consensus on the formerly nationalistic
economic regimes of the Third World. Conditions imposed in exchange
for preventing default on foreign debt included privatizing state enterprises, reduction or abolition of subsidies, opening markets to foreign

competition, and, more broadly, a shrunken role for governments. In reality, debt rises but is payable over a longer period so that annual payments are more manageable. Yet export earnings, for many, if not most of these countries, is shrinking as a result of record low commodity prices for agricultural and mineral exports. For others, earnings were down as a result of the intense competition among exporters of manufacturing products for which there is a huge overcapacity at the global level. There is precious little, if anything, for investment in future growth or even to pay for basic consumption goods like food and energy. The pressure again is on wages and working conditions as local companies squeeze workers to stay in business.

Local politics matter. In the important case of Korea, the chaebols, the giant conglomerates that dominate the economy, supported Korea's agreement with the IMF in 1998 because to them the major problem facing the country was the "excessive" power that trade unions had developed as a result of democratization a decade earlier. The IMF's insistence on the repeal of many protective labor laws and their replacement with a "fire at will" flexibility promoted policies the chaebols could not achieve on their own. Ironically many ordinary Koreans supported the IMF agreement because they believed it would break the power of the chaebols who had for decades exploited the people, supported authoritarian rule, and used their monopoly power to squash smaller businesses. The militant Korean Confederation of Trade Unions built militant resistance to the IMF's labor market restructuring demands and the neoliberal thrust of the proposal it was making to their government. Remarkably the radical unions forced the Korean government, the chaebols, and the IMF to back down, preserving jobs and existing contract protections and forcing the companies to pay a greater share of the adjustment costs.

The Agency of the American State

If the devastating effects of International Monetary Fund programs were really the accidental outcome of ill-conceived policies, as some would have it, there would be hope that IMF conditionality would have been changed long ago, since program failures and social costs have been well understood for some time. But these policies were instigated, and continue to be insisted upon, by the executive branch of the U.S. government and its European allies. The key player was Robert Rubin, secretary of the treasury and formerly the head of a major Wall Street investment bank, who spearheaded financial liberalization as the highest priority for the U.S. government's economic policy and that of the international agencies it dominates.

In its actions the Clinton administration continued the market opening policies that had long been the hallmark of U.S. strategy, but gave them new urgency in what became almost a religious crusade. As Nicholas Kristof writes with David Sanger, "Previous administrations had pushed for financial liberalization principally in Japan, but under President Clinton it became a worldwide effort directed at all kinds of countries, even smaller ones much less able to absorb it than Japan." [8] The president, wanting to make economics the centerpiece of his foreign policy, created the National Economic Council to parallel the National Security Council and put Rubin at its head. In doing so he moved the goal of financial liberalization to a top position in his government's agenda.

Jeff Garten, a former Clinton under secretary of commerce and the dean of the Yale School of Management, has spoken to interviewers about how the administration pushed "full steam ahead" on liberalization, including financial liberalization. "Wall Street was delighted that the broad trade agenda now included financial services," he said. Kristof and Sanger report, "The push for financial liberation was directed at Asia in particular, largely because it was seen as a potential gold mine for American banks and brokerages." [9] It was clear the administration obliged with little attention to the havoc its actions were producing. What explains this "carelessness"?

Both Alan Greenspan, the chair of the Federal Reserve, and influential Clinton secretary Robert Rubin were leading Wall Street figures before going into public service. Neither of them should be understood to be selfish men in the immediate sense of the word; clearly each of them would have made more money had they not gone into public service. But their socialization and the values they bring with them to public service are at issue. They came to their positions after a lifetime of making certain assumptions about the way things should work, assumptions that are part of a worldview shaped by their backgrounds. The ideas and interests that formed them continue to guide their thinking. Liberalizing capital markets has been a central goal for finance capital since political necessity in the early postwar period led to creation of the national Keynesian regimes that limited capital's mobility in favor of domestic stability and growth. Sweeping away these restrictions has been a financial sector goal ever since.

Alan Greenspan had been a J. P. Morgan director for ten years and while he was certainly philosophically disposed to repealing the Glass-Steagall Act, which had separated commercial and investment banking in the 1930s (and which resulted from disclosure of scandalous self dealing and abuse of power on Wall Street), he was also forwarding the interests of Morgan Stanley and Morgan Guaranty. Greenspan's decision to give banks permission to underwrite commercial paper and municipal revenue bonds was a boon for J. P. Morgan Securities, among others. The bank also became the first American commercial bank since the Depression to float a corporate bond issue in 1989 thanks to Greenspan's decision allowing them to do so. Such ties are important. In the case of Robert Rubin, who ran the investment bank Goldman, Sachs and Company before serving for almost all of the two terms of the Clinton presidency as secretary of the treasury, leading a campaign for global neoliberalism from a position of authority also greased the skids for repeal of the Glass-Steagall Act. The repeal was tremendously important for Citigroup, the largest U.S. financial service corporation, which calculatedly violated the act in the very act of its formation by merging the businesses of the Traveler's Group and Citicorp. It stood to gain more by the repeal of the act than any other institution. Mr. Rubin, after leaving government service, went to work as co-head of Citigroup.

The best explanation of the economic crises of the last decades of the twentieth century is the pressures for financial opening exerted by the United States, which are as effective as the gunboats of an earlier age. For those countries that experience severe crisis, there is an immediate correlation between surrendering control over their financial sector and the ensuing crises, which are widely blamed not on the forced liberalization but on "crony capitalism." Soon after countries give up their autonomy in monetary and currency policies and open their financial markets to foreign investors they experience crisis. Foreign capital initially flows in thanks to the high profitability of arbitrage—borrowing foreign funds at lower interest rates and lending them within the country at significantly higher rates. Imports of foreign goods increase; there is a building boom in office towers and luxury condominiums to house the new class of a bloated financial sector. But soon inflation comes along formed by asset bubbles from the heated speculative excesses. This produces a decline in the expected value of the currency and triggers capital flight, which, according to the rules of the bankers, requires austerity measures, which in turn lead to a rise in unemployment and mass suffering. The alternative to monetarist policies of high interest rates and contracting the money supply is an effort to reflate the economy and stimulate growth. But this cannot work in the new context. David Felix explains: "Injecting more central bank credit to bring a country out of its domestic crisis would be fruitless without a parallel restoration of import and exchange controls. Such a drastic reversal of liberalization and the rising inflation would, however, destroy any remaining confidence at home and abroad in the viability of the NL [neoliberal] experiment, which would encourage more capital flight and a still greater reluctance on the part of the foreign banks to lend." [10]

With the reflation option blocked by the constraints of neoliberalism, debtor country governments have been forced to assume responsibility for private sector debt as well as any sovereign borrowing. Neoliberal policies have now been widely tested and, judging from the recession-cum-depressions they produce, haven't worked—at least not for most citizens of the affected countries. Devaluation, the policy of choice of IMF, has not solved the problem of nonperforming loans. Imports and exports have not been very responsive to changes in exchange rates. Although elites continue to buy luxury goods, necessities become scarce and it becomes increasingly difficult to maintain basic living standards. Exports are largely unaffected because the price of commodities is set on world markets and any short-run stimulus to greater production adds to the supply, where core demand is price inelastic.

In any case, the stock markets in most of these nations are tiny compared to the amount of money poured into them. As mutual funds, pension funds, and other institutional investors piled in, share prices zoomed. So much stateless wealth is circulating to wherever those who deploy it expect high returns that booms are created, which, in the overwhelming majority of these cases, lead to speculative bubbles that collapse in what President Clinton famously described as "a few little glitches in the road here." It is said that the State Department representatives in these countries and the CIA missed the warning signs because they were used to focusing obsessive attention to communism, so could not see "the threats from business executives who wear neckties and trade currencies." But, while it may be that the State Department and the CIA do not expect problems from businessmen who wear ties and trade currencies—indeed, they are used to taking orders from such men—the great majority of the world's people have long since learned that it is just such men that they have to fear. In the present era of globalization, it is the imperialism of finance that is the most potent enemy of the people of the world.

There is an old Soviet-era joke where someone asks, "Who are the men in suits who come at the end of the May Day parade, they do not look very military." The answer is a grave "Ah, but they are the most dangerous. They are the economists." The May Day parade is gone. But today it might still seem to the average Russian citizen that those who do the most damage are those new men in the fine suits who trade currencies and the global governance men of the IMF who dispense "Washington consensus" policy advice. In the present era the economic rights of citizenship are under attack. These rights—won or expanded upon in the 1930s and the 1960s—cannot exist in a world exclusively governed by market principles. It is not that voting will be abolished. But entitlements such as health care or retirement benefits cannot be paid at levels adequate to meet basic needs under globalization. It is hardly a matter of capital versus the state, when the state is in the hands of capital, its servants and its allies. It is a matter of imperialism. While situations differ, political elites in many countries are comfortable selling their citizens to the highest bidder and transforming their location into a low tax jurisdiction to attract mobile transnational capital.

The combination of contractionary forces led to slow growth of aggregate demand that is part of the export oriented development package. It results from the destructive capacity of capital flows that keep interest rates high and state spending low. The process generates a continuing restructuring of where, how, and what is produced and begets high profit returns that, combined with the impact of income inequalities, favor elites with investable surpluses and drives asset markets to unsustainable levels. IMF's prescription that debtors impose austerity to repay foreign banks adds to deflationary pressure on the global economy by further reducing aggregate demand. The impact of these changes has produced a fragile situation for the global economy. As Ute Pieper and Lance Taylor have written, "the dramatic shifts in economic and social policy of the 1980s go far toward recreating the environment prior to the Great Depression; advocates of 'neo' liberalism say little unfamiliar from the debates of the 1920s. The world has come full circle—institutionally, ideologically, and politically." [11] As during the years leading up to the Great Depression, the majority of economists criticize all institutional impediments to free functioning markets, opposed to any attempt to stabilize an innately unstable system. Now as then, there is a great celebration of American success in a world in which there is widespread evidence that others are in serious trouble; the United States economy cannot forever be isolated from the negative consequences of these developments. While such crises were used to dismantle the challenge of nationalist development state models, we should not overly sympathize with national elites interested only in their own gains. Their bitter complaints against the IMF demanding the restructuring of their systems on terms advantageous to transnational capital ring hollow in light of their treatment of their working classes. The financial crises must be seen in the larger context of imperialist designs that use the power of the debt relationship to dominate other economies, but we also have to be aware of the class dimension of situations within countries, even as we look more carefully at the power relations between countries. It would help us understand what is going on if we speak not only of globalization but also about imperialism.

Today U.S. presidents and IMF officials have no hesitation in declaring that the benighted laggards of the world system are in need of adopting United States–style ownership laws and legal acceptance of American definitions of intellectual property. In the past non-Europeans who had not developed concepts of private property that allowed Western domination were accused of backwardness and forced to comply. Where natives proved slow learners it proved necessary "to have capitalism imposed on them. In fact, the theory was developed, mainly by lawyers and administrators in the European colonial corporations and colonial offices, and had one very concrete purpose: to establish the legal basis for expropriating land from colonized peoples, on the fiction that the colonized had no property rights to the land because they had no *concept* of property rights in land." [12] The locals today seem equally obtuse concerning the right of investors to control their resources and their culture. This may illustrate a similar embarrassing lack of understanding that cultures are merely commodities and can be owned and transformed at will by those with property rights.

Gunboats and Missiles

As a reading of Thucydides, the Greek historian of the Peloponnesian War, makes clear, military alliances have always been a vehicle for conquest and for keeping weaker allies and clients in line. In the post–Second World War period the perception of a communist threat was the rationale for supporting dictatorships in former colonial countries, where national liberation movements threatened the continuation of core-periphery dependency relationships. If U.S. meddling did not "keep the world safe for democracy," it certainly helped U.S. investment interests. With the demise of the "evil empire," continued interventions and the perpetuation of such Cold War relics as NATO and the North Atlantic Treaty Organization required new justifications. Thus categories such as "insurgency," "terrorism," and "rogue state" were invoked and, more cynically, "human rights," as occasion, for increasing numbers of "power projections" as the Pentagon called its global policing missions. The United States under President Clinton escalated policies evident under his predecessors, and claimed the right and responsibility to intervene everywhere wherever "our interests are at stake" and where "we could make a difference." As he announced in a February 26, 1999, speech in San Francisco: "It's easy . . . to say that we really have no interest in who lives in this or that valley in Bosnia, or who owns a strip of brushland in the Horn of Africa, or some piece of parched earth by the Jordan River. But the true measure of our interests lies not in how small or distant these places are, or in whether we have trouble pronouncing their names. The question we must ask is, what are the consequences to our security of letting conflicts fester and spread. We cannot, indeed, we should not, do anything or be everywhere. But," the president went on making the new world order nature of his analysis clear, "where our values and our interests are at stake, and where we can make a difference, we must be prepared to do so."

Michael Klare calls this proposition that the best way to maintain stability is to intervene before problems intensify and spread, the Clinton Doctrine. It is surely the most far-reaching and ambitious policy announced by any American president since the Vietnam War. It suggested that the bombing of Yugoslavia would be only one of a series of recurring projections or threats of force.[13] Clinton's secretary of state told a December 1998 NATO foreign ministers meeting in Brussels that "Common sense tells us that it is sometimes better to deal with instability when it is still at arm's length than to wait until it is at our doorstep," as though Slobodan Milosevic was poised to invade Virginia Beach.

In its effort to turn NATO from a defensive alliance protecting Europe in the unlikely event of Soviet invasion, the United States was transforming NATO into a rapid deployment vehicle that would militarily intervene in the affairs of sovereign nations when their internal policies did not meet with United States approval. As one editorial writer suggested: "Washington can now cite NATO's new strategic concept to justify virtually any attack it wishes to wage against any nation. Take note: We are here at the creation of a global NATO intervention force." [14] This transformation of NATO's mission was disturbing to many establishment figures because it placed such obvious stress on the military face of U.S. imperialism. A *New York Times* editorial warned, for example, against "transforming the alliance into a global strike force against American and European interests." [15]

Benjamin Schwarz and Christopher Layne presented America's Balkan interventions in the context of U.S. economic interest:

> The air war in Serbia is just the latest installment in what appears to be Washington's quest to make the world safe for American investors and exporters. Last

year [1999], speaking to the Boston Chamber of Commerce, Defense Secretary William Cohen justified NATO expansion as a way of "spreading the kind of security and stability that Western Europe has enjoyed since World War II to Central and Eastern Europe. And with that spread of stability, there is a prospect to attract investment." No doubt the Administration is moved by the human tragedy in Kosovo. Clearly, however, its perception that U.S. economic interests are indirectly at stake is at least as important. As Cohen has said, the Administration's strategy seeks to "discourage violence and instability—instability which destroys lives and markets." Clinton recently exhorted Americans to accept the "inevitable logic" of globalism and free trade. But the Administration's Balkan policy shows that globalization is not inevitable—it depends on America's overseas military commitments and its willingness to wage war if necessary. [16]

It is also useful to remember that the now former Yugoslavia was one of the formerly socialist countries in which the transition to United States–style free market capitalism was particularly strongly resisted by a working class majority. The strongmen, Franjo Tudjman in Croatia and Slobodan Milosevic in Serbia, were in the service of the IMF restructuring of their political economies. The economic policies they embraced led to massive declines in living standards, produced economic chaos, and motivated militant strikes. Serbian President Milosevic used ultra-nationalism to divide the powerful working-class opposition. Ethnic hatred became state policy and the atrocities that followed must be seen in this context.

The military industry in the United States was a major lobbyist for NATO expansion. A Lockheed Martin executive heads the Committee to Expand NATO, the main lobbying force, and other military contractors have lavished funds on the NATO expansion effort. This is only good business sense. U.S. arms manufacturers can expect $35 billion over the first decade of the new millennium as a result of NATO expansion.[17] Any country that joins is committed to spending 3 percent of its budget on the military and, to fulfill requirements for compatibility, is likely to buy its armaments from these same sponsors. It is difficult to know how much military intervention is a result of geopolitical strategy and how much simply subsidizes the arms industry, which contributes heavily to politicians. The interpenetration of narrow material interests and wider system-supporting imperial design obfuscates any conflicts of interest.

Arms sales are important to examine, because they create the very violence that the United States uses as an excuse to step into a conflict. Of the twenty-four countries that experienced at least one armed conflict in 1997 (the most recent year for which data is available at this writing), the United States sold weapons and/or provided military training to twenty-one of them at some point during the 1990s. Exceptions such as Iran and Afghanistan received major arms shipments and extensive training in previous decades. [18] Most weapons exports originate from the United States, facilitating the same violence that the United States moralistically condemns whenever it wants a pretext for humanitarian interventions. It was not only the financial aspects of globalization that unleashed the particular instabilities of the late twentieth and early twenty-first centuries. The classic instrumentalities of imperial violence are hardly absent from the globalized political economy's functioning. As Ellen Meiksins Wood writes:

> If today's imperialism does not typically express itself in direct military domination of colonies, this does not mean that it is any less militaristic than the old variety. The point is certainly not that the world is more peaceful because the old principles of military conquest have given way to less violent means of commerce and financial domination. On the contrary, military force is still central to the imperialist project, in some ways more than ever. But now it has to be used in different ways and with different objectives. [19]

Whether the protesters in the streets of Seattle and at other demonstrations against the reign of the global financial institutions will have occasion to connect the economic policies of transnational capital to the wars that plague so many poor countries remains to be seen. The movement for global, social justice has been able to a remarkable degree to spread a broad awareness of how economic weapons are used by these institutions to limit the life chances of the peoples of the world. Whether the movement develops a broader anti-imperialist critique is an open question.

CHAPTER FIVE

Miracles and Crises in the Southeast Asian Economies

So far globalization has been analyzed mainly in its broadly historical outlines. This is a necessary starting point in as, all too often, the process of globalization is seen as the inevitable consequence of technologies with no precedent, an overturning of historical patterns. Opposing this view, the analyses made in previous chapters—of the consolidation of national and global markets over the past century or more, of the changing form of the state in the aftermath of the depression of the 1930s and the Second World War, and of the ways in which powerful states such as the United States have used global finance to dominate others—have been intended to show that contemporary globalization is rooted in processes that have always been the focus of political contestation, and whose history we ignore at our own peril. But the analysis of globalization needs not only to be developed historically, but must be tested against more specific recent events if it is to demonstrate its capacity to clarify our own context and explain its causes. In this chapter we look in greater detail at perhaps the most widely discussed financial crisis of the late twentieth century and consider the debate over its causes.

We will explore the way that the United States used international state governance institutions to impose economic and political changes on some of the most successful developing economies in world history.

Such "solutions" were successful impositions of imperial designs on weaker states, especially those that had been successful in achieving a relative autonomy pursuing national development state capital alternatives to the usual pattern of foreign domination. Demonstrations for debt forgiveness have focused on the poorest of the poor who were most clearly unable to pay debt and whose prospects were so grim when their limited resources were siphoned off in debt repayment without hope of ever getting out of bondage. The inability to fund basic education and health care due to the debt burden prompted a powerful worldwide movement of conscience for debt relief. This will be discussed in the final chapter. In this chapter, we focus on the richer and most successful of the developing economies, those of East Asia. We do so to highlight the ways in which the global state economic governance institutions and the international financiers that they represent are responsible in significant measure for causing and worsening financial crises in that region. Although the chapter focuses specifically on East Asia, the patterns it identifies are relevant—to different degrees, and with historical variations—in other contexts as well.

Financial Crisis in East Asia

East Asia, with about a quarter of the world's output, accounted for half of global growth in the 1990s and two-thirds of the world's capital spending—until around 1997. Then financial crisis struck. At first it was said that the problem would be of short duration. In July 1997, the Asian Development Bank's chief economist predicted these economies "should be growing at a fair clip" in the second half of 1998 and thereafter. In October 1997 Stanley Fisher, the first deputy managing director of the International Monetary Fund, at the fifty-first annual meeting of the IMF and World Bank in Hong Kong, said, "Our experience has been that this sort of crisis lasts three or four months." Alan Greenspan, speaking at the annual convention of the American Society of Newspaper Editors in April 1998, presented the crisis as a hiccup in the "inexorable trend toward market capitalism and political systems that stress the rule of law." He saw the crisis as insignificant in the larger historical perspective.

The dominant interpretation of the problems encountered by the Asian economies was that they were downed by "crony capitalism"; it was excessive governmental control that had been the basic problem. It was widely believed that ending interventionist state policies and a greater transparency and reliance on free markets would set matters right. More critical voices blamed financial liberalization as leading to a speculative bubble and blamed international investors for taking advantage of the regional crisis to pick up assets at low cost, and to force changes that the countries in question had been unwilling to make until compelled by a crisis situation. According to Greenspan and other spokespersons for America's brand of capitalism, the crisis was about the disciplinary power of markets forcing governments to adopt the U.S. model of capitalism. In this regard the crisis was an opportunity for "us" as much as it was a crisis for "them."

The United States had long sought to open these economies in which national developmental state industrial policies have excluded American firms, part of a strategy that produced the most rapid growth rates the world had ever known. By demanding that outsiders be allowed to compete on equal terms, the United States and the international financiers were asking for a radical reorienting of these economies, the abandonment of a successful economic model, and the imposition of severe dislocations and loss of social cohesion.

The output losses from the East Asian financial crisis from 1998 to 2000 were estimated at nearly $2 trillion (an amount double the current income of the poorest fifth of the world's population). It was paid in loss of livelihood for tens of millions, dramatically rising poverty, small business bankruptcy, reduced health care and schooling for families under stress, and ineffectual governments who were suddenly unable to meet the modest obligations they had assumed. The recovery since the nadir of the fall of 1998 was in gains in output growth, exchange rate strength, and balance of payments improvements. As in past crises these macroeconomic balances can recover fairly quickly but it takes considerably longer for employment and wages to regain their earlier levels. An analysis of 80 countries over roughly the last quarter of the twentieth century and the 300 economic crises they experienced shows that output growth recovers to pre-crisis levels in one year on average after the peak of the problem period but income distribution worsens for three years and real wage growth takes about four years to recover. [1] As in the case of the Latin American debt crisis in the 1980s, which was "solved" by a lost decade—by the end, the working class and peasantry of the continent were in worse shape than they had been at the start of the crisis, but economies had been transformed and were now opened to foreign capital on U.S. terms—so in Asia American policy makers insisted on solutions that many considered to be in the best interests of transnational capital rather than the people of the region. Profits recovered, but the crisis produced sustained effects that have not been kind to the working class of the region.

Regional leaders blamed the financial opening that the West, especially the United States and the IMF, urged upon them. Too much capital flowed in too fast and then, at the sign of a downturn, fled even faster. And while capital markets are subject to waves of over optimism and then extreme pessimism, some regional leaders, most famously Mahathir Mohamed, accused the Jews, George Soros in particular, and the hedge funds in general, of trying to destroy Malaysia's economy. "For them wealth must come from impoverishing others," he said. He declared currency trading "unnecessary, unproductive, and immoral" and proceeded to end the convertibility of his country's currency. While most mainstream economists thought such a step would be a disaster, a year later when the crisis had passed and the controls were lifted when it turned out that no harm was done to the Malaysian economy, there was an emerging sense that controls against speculative and destabilizing short-term hot money flows might not be a bad idea.

This chapter will discuss potential consequences to adapting one or another of the various approaches to the East Asian financial crisis, especially examining the role of the International Monetary Fund's structural adjustment demands on the region. There has been widespread disapproval of the IMF role, including comments from representatives of the World Bank, which was openly critical of the IMF-imposed austerity measures and the structural adjustments that were demanded. Along with others, the World Bank was concerned about the growing political unrest as a result of the harshness of the IMF's approach. Others worried, correctly as it turned out, that the deflationary pressures that IMF cures imposed on the Asian countries would spread recession rather than contain crisis.

Background to the Crisis

Philip Golub expressed a view shared by others when he wrote, "By imposing a draconian purge on countries that have already been bled white, the international financial institutions and markets are reinventing the suicidal policy of the early 1930s." [2] He notes that while officials should have given themselves some monetary room for maneuver to cushion the shock of the 1929 crash, the central banks of the United Kingdom, Germany, and the United States instead squeezed credit even further. The consequences are well known. Referring to Chancellor Bruening's deflationary policy, the Reichsbank chairman at the time, Hans Luther, said there was no other solution. "The dominant thinking is no different today." [3] We will wait for history's verdict of course, and so far this historical parallel has been a groundless fear, but even without the wider implications, the local impacts of austerity were severe for millions of the region's workers, small business people, and farmers.

The national regimes of the region were created in the Cold War climate of the post–Second World War years in which the United States supported and sometimes directly installed congenial regimes, usually headed by military strongmen willing to suppress opposition and to massacre those who resisted their rule (as in Taiwan, South Korea, Indonesia and elsewhere). In an effort to gain legitimacy through economic growth, these regimes were accorded privileges and foreign aid by the United States as part of its Cold War strategy. The redistributions and planning of the communist regimes in China and North Korea were met by land reform and state-sponsored industrialization in Taiwan and South Korea along lines very different from the free market model the Americans insisted be followed elsewhere. These "front line" states were considered primarily in geopolitical terms rather than as venues for immediate exploitation, as was the case in Latin America, for example. The leading "economic miracles" of the region owe much to Cold War considerations.

If there is, or was, an East Asian development model, a conjecture that is hotly debated, it is in the widely held agreement that state power can be used to help national capital compete in global markets by protecting local firms from foreign competition, providing them with low-cost capital for productive investment, preventing funds that are needed for domestic investment from draining abroad either into higher return foreign investments or into excessive luxury imports, and holding down labor costs by whatever means. Local banks are seen as conduits, mobilizing domestic savings and allowing national capital to expand continuously without risk that loans will be called or borrowing costs increased. Foreign banks were prevented from either entering or playing a major role in a nation's economy so that these conditions could be maintained. Repressive governments prevented independent labor unions or oppositional political movements and kept the consumption of the masses to a minimum so that accumulation would be maximized.

State-led development, using below market financing and high leverage, successfully built industrial capacity capable of breaking the industrial monopoly of core producers. The first to do so— Japan, South Korea and Taiwan—were encouraged as we have noted by the United States for geopolitical reasons. In those years, the threat of communist China trumped the usual American determination to avoid Third World industrialization. With time, the prospects of low cost manufacturing in the region as a source of potential profitability for United States–based transnationals changed the strategic outlook of the American state. National capitals in the region took advantage of this opening to assert substantial control over their country's development. Other, weaker nations were mere export platforms for U.S. and Japanese transnationals.

For decades, government-sponsored development used banking as a vehicle for the statist developmental strategy (complete with political patronage and economic corruption, which did not seem to be a serious handicap until external conditions changed). Banks, by mobilizing resources on a massive scale and allocating them at low cost to favored industries, allowed these countries to enter world industrial markets as producers. The high leverage was the tool of national development policy.[4] This Asian economic model, which for three decades moved more people out of poverty faster than ever before in the history of capitalism, is now convicted in the eyes of many economists on the very basis of its past success: "the trinity of over-investment, over-spending, and over-guidance." [5]

The accumulation regime foundered on two unyielding rocks. The first was global overcapacity. The second was the collapse of the financial bubbles that were produced when expanded productive investment opportunities could no longer be found for the vast savings these economies generated and, as it turned out, more importantly to foreign borrowing that their success encouraged. As funds that could not be invested productively found their way into property and stock market speculation, as well as corrupt borrowing by companies whose only claim to new loans was their political power to extort them, a bubble of excess grew and inevitably burst. A global economy values growth through exports, which places a premium on lowering costs of production rather than, as in the era of national Keynesianism, stimulating growth by increasing aggregate demand. Thus the cures for economic crisis at the end of the twentieth century impart a strong deflationary bias to the world system.

As it became clear that the world could not absorb all of the potential production, the high debt ratios that had been used to finance the overinvestment became unsustainable, undermining the financial viability of businesses throughout the region. The speculative fever that had driven real estate and share markets was similarly based on expectations that markets could only continue to go up and that the wise investor would know when to exit to avoid disaster should they peak—something all speculators never, of course, do. Deflation, if it spread, could become serious. Gently falling prices are one thing. But there is potential for financial overextension triggering a spiral of competitive devaluations stemming from an inability to rationalize and restructure overproduction and debt in a truly timely fashion. It is the combination of foreign borrowing that cannot be sustained and the great difficulty in perpetuating the export model due to cost squeeze and market saturation that sets the stage for the serious rise in unemployment and the fiscal crisis of states of the region unable to address social needs created by the economic downturn. The crisis brought on by forced

liberalization and lack of adequate social controls becomes the leverage
for the IMF and other global institutions to demand more deregulation,
privatization, and erosion of progressive government-financed social
programs. The crisis in Asia allowed foreign capital to buy assets in the
region at distress prices. "Handled well," the resulting concentration
and centralization of economic power will result in "solving" the Asian
crisis by foreign transnational corporations gaining greater control over
the region, opening markets that had long been protected. Most scenarios call for a restructuring of debt in Latin American fashion, increasing
foreign ownership and imposing austerity. Recovery requires the return
to profitability for private corporations, writing down asset values and
other measures that lower costs and subsidize profitability.

The Specters of Deflation and Overcapacity

In 1998 Japan witnessed deflation, the United States and other
advanced economies had the lowest measured inflation in decades, and
most of the rest of Asia saw plummeting stock and property markets
and falling incomes and asset values. Excess capacity in products from
steel and auto production to memory chips and gas turbines created
gloom-and-doom forecasts. In the chemical industry, Asian producers
continued, for example, to increase ethylene (a plastics building block)
by 70 percent, despite the region's financial problems. The financial
press is full of such examples. The Asian financial crisis coincided with
global overcapacity. "Pricing pressures are dramatic across sector after
sector," said GE Chairman Jack Welch. "There is excess global capacity
in almost every industry." [6] The crisis meant that these nations were
forced to cut their imports and to step up exports even if this required
dramatically lower prices—which put further downward pressure on
profit per unit sold.

The export oriented development model demanded by the IMF and
WB produced global underconsumptionist pressures. Each country, in
trying to increase its exports, worked to keep its labor costs down, which
affected domestic purchasing power and standards of living. As opposed
to the national Keynesian model in which wage growth and government
social spending created demand, global neoliberalism looks for markets

abroad and insists on austerity at home. When many countries pursue the same logic, given the constraints on mass purchasing power, the result is overcapacity. It becomes difficult to sell all that can be produced. The luxury market does grow, thanks to the perverse income distribution that accompanies the model, but wealth is funneled into speculative investment to a significant degree rather than adequately supporting markets for goods and services.

While academics have been slow to take up this issue, there has been increasing debate among bankers, central bankers, and other members of the financial community and among some policy makers. The two major positions on the issue are reflected in the financial press. *Business Week* suggested there was no reason to worry.

> Deflation in the 1990s is uncharted territory. In the '30s, it destroyed income and jobs, eviscerated savings, and kept the world poor from 1929 until World War II. Yet in this decade, deflation has led to high growth and rising real wages as high-tech companies cut costs, raise productivity, and increase unit sales to compensate for falling prices. The big question is whether this can work for the entire global economy. Will there come a point when increases in productivity and unit sales fail to outpace falling prices, triggering a deflationary spiral? With U.S. producer prices down 0.4 percent for the year and inflation approaching zero, we may soon get an answer.[7]

That other major financial periodical, the *Economist,* disagreed, taking the conventional neoclassical economic position that "Deflation, when it happens, exposes not the flaw in capitalism but the incompetence of central banks and governments."[8] One need not defend the capitalist state or a disinterested wisdom on the part of its central bankers to note that the objective conditions under which they operate encourage certain choices, which, although free market advocates may not like it, are part of the logic that it is the project of the *Economist* to deny. The normal workings of the capitalist system create speculative bubbles and always have. Central bankers are faced with scenarios in which the only way to produce growth is to create conditions that will, further down the line, lead to overexpansion and recession/depression. Such financial cycles are an endogenous part of the system as it has always operated. The stronger the free market ideology, the more extreme these cycles are likely to be. It is trust in the stability of unregulated markets that is the problem and not the solution. For this reason central bankers meet in Basel to devise, as best they can, safeguards for the international financial system, so that unregulated capitalism does not bring new disasters upon the system. The East Asian financial crisis can be seen in the context of the growing importance of international capital markets in reshaping economic relations and of a financial instability.

The problem, as we have seen repeatedly, is that on a global basis excess liquidity seeking high short-term returns courses through financial markets in eventually destabilizing patterns. In this process regulators extend guarantees to "protect" financial institutions, which allows them to take greater future risks, fostering greater systematic instability as a result. If we think of the measure of global excess money as broad money growth minus nominal GDP growth—the funds available to invest in financial markets—we should be worried, because by such measures liquidity has grown well beyond sustainable bounds in a system given to greater propensity toward high stakes financial gambles. This money finds its way into asset markets (especially property and stock markets), bidding prices up.

But even if there are worries about inflation in financial markets, there is scarcely any inflation these days in real markets (price stability or deflation is more the pattern), and so if monetary authorities were to choose to put on the brakes by raising interest rates, this would hurt the real economy of goods, services, jobs, and industrial and commercial profits. If authorities do not intervene, as was the case in Thailand, Hong Kong, and other places where asset prices got out of line, a bubble economy develops and deflates in widely painful ways.

The Crisis Story

The accepted interpretation of the East Asian financial crisis is that banks and non-financial corporations in these countries borrowed in dollars at low interest rates and invested domestically, obtaining high returns. This continued as long as investors believed that their currencies would not lose value so that the dollar and yen debts could be repaid. Given the commitment of local Asian governments to maintaining the value of their currencies, their longstanding growth, and proven ability to defend their currencies, capital flowed in. When growth slowed and debt refinancing became problematic, the speculative bubble in stock and property markets burst. The whole thing fell apart. Banks became insolvent along with many of the largest and formerly most successful corporations. So much is agreed upon.

Over the years 1995 to 1997 the dollar rose in value by about 50 percent against the Japanese yen. Countries that had tied the value of their currency to the dollar therefore saw their currencies appreciate and the price of their goods go up, reducing their export competitiveness. As their economy slowed, debt burdens increased, and their property boom became shaky. Investment slowed and the balance of payments deficits grew. The pressure led to devaluation of currencies, so refinancing dollar-denominated debt increased dramatically at the same time as repayment ability weakened substantially. Bankruptcies followed. Thailand had foreign obligations that exceeded 4 percent of its GDP for a half-dozen years preceding its crisis, but it was only when growth slowed that investors became concerned. They rushed to protect their capital, getting as much out of the baht as fast as they could. Governments in such a condition could try and defend their currency's value by offering higher and higher interest rates to compensate lenders for possible devaluation. But such high interest rates, 50 percent or more, were difficult for domestic industry to pay. Further, local banks were hesitant to lend at any interest rate at all. They had so many bad loans that they needed to build up reserves. Local companies with contracts to export could not honor them because they could not get short-term loans to finance production and export of their products. This "credit crunch" destroyed basically healthy businesses as well as weak ones. It is at this point that we started to hear so much about "crony capitalism." Many of the bad loans had been made to politically connected borrowers often without adequate collateral, or any collateral. Banks went bankrupt and demanded government bailouts since the lending had been at the request of the politicians and other officials.

For a year or so preceding the collapse of the bath, Thailand had been urged by the IMF to reduce its short-term borrowing and do something about its banking system and its speculative lending practices. The early warning system that the IMF had so proudly put in place after the Mexican peso crisis in 1995 failed because, although the IMF gave the early warning to Thailand, the Thai leaders who were making money hand over fist were not inclined to listen. Local elites understood that the basic rule of capitalism is to get rich. They did. They denied anything was wrong for as long as they possibly could. Since other countries in the region had been following basically similar practices they too were vulnerable and a domino effect or financial "contagion" spread. Thailand's problems, it turned out, were part of a larger context of overcapacity, the inability of the Asian miracle economies to sell enough even at lower prices to finance their corporate borrowing. Further, just as the East Asian economies had taken over labor-intensive commodity manufacturing from high-wage Western nations, China increasingly undercut the Thais and other East Asian producers. Thailand had borrowed more than other East Asian export regimes as a percentage of its GDP, the proxy for its ability to finance debt, and so crisis struck there first. But the bubble economy could not outlast the global slowdown and the overinvestment and asset speculation it produced.

Some investors claim they did not know the "real situation." They call for better and timelier information and "greater transparency," a phrase that seems to mean that Asian businesses should use United States–style accounting and disclosure standards. Yet it seems clear that investors asked few questions. They were attracted by expected high returns and pushed by low returns at home. Surely the way these economies operated did not change. For example, in Indonesia, one of the hardest hit, growth had been a steady 6 to 8 percent a year for a decade. The banks lent to whomever the government told them to, including the children of the Indonesian dictator who also chose most of the members of the parliament, which was a rubber stamp affair. He also appointed the upper ranks within the military that ran the country. Until the early 1980s, the banks were in fact state owned. After that interest rates were freed, new licenses given out, and private banks proliferated.

By the early 1990s bank credit was expanding by about 50 percent a year, clearly an unsustainable situation. Non-performing loans grew but there was little or no regulation of the banks and losses could easily be covered up. Indonesia was not the only country where losses were hidden and bogus figures published. Accounting rules throughout the region are weak and enforcement weaker or nonexistent. As in Russia and much of Latin America as well as Korea and elsewhere in East Asia, loan classification rules were, and continue to be, "adaptable." Banks appear to be making good profits up to the moment they are threatened with closure. Large financial groups that guarantee loans for other companies have huge, but non-disclosed, exposures. As long as growth continues none of this really matters. When growth slows the high debt ratios become unsustainable. Private foreign capital, which had flowed in so freely, crowds the door in a mad rush to exit the weakening economy, dramatically worsening the situation. The panic punishes the economy to a far more severe extent than its "fundamentals" would seem to call for, but panic does not respect such subtleties.

While newspaper accounts focused on the loss to investors and ran human-interest stories about the "new poor" having dumped their BMWs on the market at distress prices, millions of desperate small business, self-employed, and industrial workers were also victimized by the events. It is they who pay the highest price for the opportunism of the elites. The IMF austerity programs devastate the people, but pay off the banks as the price of the promise that the music will start again. The promise of the IMF is that the game can continue once the shakeout takes place. With each round of forced liberalization, the transnational corporations and global finance tighten their grip.

The Debate

Mainstream financial theory rests on what is known as the Modigliani-Miller proposition. It asserts that the capital structure of a firm—the mix of equity and debt on its balance sheet—doesn't matter. Modigliani-Miller claims that the market value of any firm is independent of its capital structure. For many East Asian economies this seemed to be wrong. The high debt levels of companies meant that any slowdown dramatically increased their fixed costs since, unlike stockholders who can be put off with low or no dividends, bond holders must be paid on time and in full. As long as companies were profitably expanding, such high leverage made sense. It allowed faster expansion. Local companies were in a position to undertake high-risk, potentially high return projects that required large amounts of capital, for example chip factories, which cost a billion dollars or so each. But when economic growth slows the debt burden can become intolerable. Governments, so long as they were able to keep financial markets closed to capital flight, could weather crises by backing loans made and keeping companies afloat through periods of negative cash flow until economic recovery allowed restarting debt repayment. Government guarantees thus allowed more risk in the system than otherwise would have been possible—and higher growth. Loans were made not because of the viability of particular projects but because lenders felt more protected against loss by such implicit state guarantees. In the 1990s, under pressure from international finance and the United States, governments that opened financial markets lost considerable control over their economies.

The supporters of state-led growth argue that it is financial liberalization (which allows free short-term capital flows) that has produced the region's liquidity problems and undermined the high debt system that has been so effective. Without the government being able to stop short-term capital flight, debtors are unable to continue to finance their obligations. Open capital markets in a period of slow growth have effectively undermined the system that has for decades produced record growth. The most extreme case is perhaps that of Korea where the sales of the top four chaebols—the conglomerates that like the Japanese keiretsus after which they are modeled, own a wide variety of businesses from consumer electronics to steel mills to banks—generate half of the country's exports. They depend on very high leverage and continuous expansion to legitimize borrowing which in turn depends on increasing exports. Any break in expansion means diminished capacity to meet interest payments and makes rolling-over borrowing more difficult. When Korea's growth rate fell from an outstanding 9 percent in 1995 to a still quite remarkable 6 percent in 1996, the slowdown was accompanied by a doubling in the country's trade deficit. In its state-controlled system Korea's widely used short-term debt instruments, predominantly three- and six-month promissory notes (OUM) which are typically continuously rolled over, planners who strongly influenced bank lending practices had a powerful lever with which to direct national development. They could exercise displeasure at particular corporations whose policy choices displeased them by discouraging rollover of their OUM falling due. The system was more complicated in that companies used OUM rather than cash to pay each other and firms could take these promissory notes to banks for discounting should they need cash. So many of these notes were in circulation that they represented a huge burden on the system should they not be honored. The rising number of bankruptcies Korea experienced from 1997 reflected just this occurrence.

The Korean government has felt popular pressure to rein in the chaebol whose monopoly position—expansion for growth's sake and predatory practices toward smaller firms—had increasingly slowed Korea's growth and threatened its future. However, the reformer President Kim Dae Young was unable to make much progress given a legislature beholden to bank and chaebol interests that financed a majority in the national assembly. That majority was not about to bite the hand that fed them. As a consequence, there was no significant progress with corporate governance standards, accounting transparency, or an end to cross-lending guarantees for subsidiaries and affiliates. By the fall of 1998, industrial production has fallen by almost 50 percent and unemployment was above 10 percent and rising in a country with little in the way of a safety net and small chance of finding new employment.

Certainly most Koreans believed that their system needed reform. Most citizens in Southeast Asia, the MIT countries (Malaysia, Indonesia, and Thailand), held similar views of the need to change their governments. The suffering that the crisis caused made people more intolerant of the lack of democracy and accountability of ruling elites. Still a question remains as to whether the West led by the United States had the right to impose changes in this moment of crisis, changes that are in the interests of Western capital, even as they represent a commitment to democratic reform. This debate was particularly heated in the instance of Korea, which had democratized and was struggling with reforming its economy. The pressure that the United States put on Korea was seen as an effort on the part of U.S. capital to profit from Korean problems rather than a sincere effort to offer help. The IMF and American policy makers on the other hand said that the deregulation they insisted upon was necessary for the good of Korea.

The crisis was the occasion to effectively pressure Korea to sell off assets to foreign capital. The demands for trade liberalization and further loosening of capital account freedoms are likely to be counter-productive and painful in the short run. The demand that Korea trans-form its economy in an "Anglo-Saxon direction" was a call to surrender autonomy and fall in line with the global changes being demanded by transnational corporate capital led by the International Monetary Fund and the executive branch of the United States government in negotia-tions with debtor states. One can say that Korea's problems were "po-litical," but there was more at stake; the demand was for the dismantling of the developmental model that had served Korea well for decades of record growth, rather than a push to democratize it.

In Southeast Asia, in the MIT countries, the case was easier to make that crony capitalism had prevented better adjustment to the interna-tional financial crisis. But again the causes could be found in the extremes of foreign capital flows, speculative excess, and overcapacity. And here too growth covered up corrupt practices, which were suddenly exposed when exports slumped. The corrupt, repressive regimes of Asia, Africa, and Latin America were the creatures of the Cold War period when the United States supported dictatorship as a bulwark against communist-led popular movements. These regimes kept the red men-ace at bay. In the post–Cold War era they are expendable, no longer needed after the demise of communism. Globalization now allows, and benefits from, dismantling these corrupt, rent-seeking regimes. Rule of law and more honest enforcement of contracts, the end of extortionist practices by local officials, and the favoring of domestic elites in the marketplace are in the interest of transnational capital. The Southeast Asian crisis represented an opportunity to transform these regimes. The cost of recovery, as the costs of restructuring in Western and Eastern Europe and elsewhere, would be paid through great austerity and increased working-class sacrifice.

The Causes of the Crisis

In general, there are two competing explanations of what caused the Asian crisis. The first blames the way capital markets operate. The second faults the way the East Asian states function. In the first argument, excessive liquidity in the world's capital markets plays the key role. The low returns in the core countries lead to overenthusiastic financial investment in East Asia. In some accounts it was the lack of transparency in Asian regulatory regimes that obscured the high risks involved. In others, the foreign investors set aside any tests of creditworthiness and simply piled in without proper evaluation of the risks involved. The two versions need not be contradictory of course. Both are correct in their view that fundamentally it was a market problem. The cheap capital made borrowing attractive and lenders failed to add up the exposure of those to whom they were lending. Markets did not evaluate risk properly and financial crisis resulted. But this is the nature of financial markets. They swing from overoptimism to overpessimism, creating severe cyclical contractions. The conventional view is that markets are rational and given proper information price assets correctly. The problem with the conventional view is that information must be interpreted and subjectivity is paramount. Mass psychology and herd behavior are powerful forces.

The second approach blames the governments involved for their development state policies of "centralized, bureaucratic control" and "crony capitalism," which meant that loans were made by domestic banks on the basis of government influence without proper regard for the risks involved. The availability of low-cost capital led to overinvestment by companies focused on growth rather than returns. Other lending was for speculative and for low return, ill-conceived projects that—when economic growth slowed—could not support repayments. This second approach sees recovery as demanding a transformation of the way these economies do business, giving up on bad loans and asset write-downs and opening up markets so that assets can be sold at realistic prices to those willing and able to buy. This, of course, means foreigners, since the banks and corporations are illiquid or insolvent.

While those who see the deregulation of financial markets to blame for the crisis want more serious international regulation of capital flows, those who hold to the state failure view want to deregulate the East Asian economies and give control to markets. Critics of the blame-the-market theory admit that efficient markets need government supervision, but only to the extent that market participants are well informed and treated fairly. They blame governments for preventing markets from working efficiently. Critics of this blame-the-government explanation say that all successful industrializations in the past were based on state intervention, low-cost capital, subsidies, and the other market distortions that the East Asian economies used quite successfully for decades. Moreover, to attempt to identify the state as producing inefficient outcomes and the market as the only way to attain correct prices ignores the need for short-term protection and subsidy to jump-start growth and also fails to appreciate that domestic capitalists are deeply involved in the system. It is not one that "governments" impose on private investors, but rather is the way capitalism works. Doing away with regulation does not produce efficient operation but instead produces powerful forms of rent seeking that must be addressed by state regulation.

The central conflict among interpreters of the East Asian financial crisis then is between those who put their faith in free markets and criticize governments that do not allow markets to function freely and those who see the need for a development state to organize economies and set rules within which markets should function. American policy makers and economists generally are on the "let the free market do it" side. Asian policy makers generally have seen a key role for state guidance and control. Both have been shaken by recent events. Laissez-faire is seen to have its problems and state bureaucrats have proven far from infallible. To blame government is short-sighted. Such episodes of overinvestment, unsustainable growth, and then collapse are all too familiar in the history of the global system. They have always been the occasion for a substantial redistribution of wealth as those with the deepest pockets are able to increase their ownership claims at a substantial discount. It is of course natural for capital to blame the errors on the part of regulators for the failures; this increases capital's leverage on the state that would constrain its actions.

We come then to the competing analyses of what should be done. The disparate positions of the many economists and political scientists, government officials, and international organizations reflect very different understandings of how to balance the various factors that have contributed to the crisis. At one extreme are those who see the problems as brought on by the countries themselves. Another perspective blames the international organizations and the United States for forcing a deregulation of financial markets that produced the crisis. This second position argues that these economies were in pretty decent shape and that no change had occurred that called for the massive loss of confidence the region has suffered. If we accept the first explanation, then control of financial markets and more extensive regulation of capital flows and oversight are called for. If we focus on the second position, then greater transparency and freer markets to permit cost-reducing competition and writing down of overvalued assets are in order. Reforms along both lines are likely. The questions are who will regulate international finance and how? If assets are to be written down how will this happen and who will end up controlling them, and at what price? There are also less frequently asked questions. What role will working people in these countries come to play in determining the future of their economic and political system? How will the struggle for free trade unions and fair elections progress? These questions will be answered not by economic theory but as a result of political struggles.

These political struggles go on within countries and between countries and in dealing with international financial institutions. One of the reasons the Japanese financial crisis continued for so long is that while there was agreement that the banks needed to write down hundreds of billions of dollars of non-performing loans and companies needed to sell off bad assets, powerful interests resisted taking losses. In the case of the largest problem bank, the Long Term Investment Bank, the ruling Liberal Democratic party (LDP) wanted, and received, a taxpayer bailout. The opposition wanted to nationalize the bank before any taxpayer funds were extended and put the bank under new management. The bank had been a central conduit for LDP supporters, for example the powerful rural cooperatives, a major supporter of the party that had huge amounts tied up in the bank that they could have lost if equity holders were forced to take losses under the opposition's plan. Voters were upset, but the power of money politics is such that real opposition in Japan is limited to the communist party—all others are tainted by pervasive corruption.

Again the International Monetary Fund

There is a similar problem when we again consider International Monetary Fund loans that bailed out debtors and creditors in countries from Thailand to Russia. Should the IMF continue to lend to countries that have become bankrupt? The IMF charter calls on it to aid countries experiencing temporary problems. But the IMF has moved into a lender of last resort for economies with deep structural problems. What reforms can be justified as the price of such aid? Since it is widely believed that it is unrealistic to think these debtors can work out their problems without assistance, and managing default settlements would be so very messy without coordination, the role for foreign governments and international agencies seems clear. But this begs the question, what kind of role? The IMF accepts that the advanced economies and global financial markets "contributed significantly" to the buildup of the East Asian crisis. Weak growth in Europe and Japan since the beginning of the 1990s, Stanley Fisher, IMF's first managing director, has explained, led investors to seek higher returns in East Asia's fast-growing economies. The carry trade, borrowing at low interest rates in core currencies and lending in East Asia at high rates, represented, in Fisher's words, "an imprudent search for high yields by international investors without due regard for potential risks." Too true—in hindsight. But vast fortunes were made in this carry trade. It is hardly a new strategy and it always carries risk that the underlying conditions that make it possible will change. Pious talk of lack of prudence is cheap. The system encourages such behavior and regulators are too cowardly to challenge it. New "reforms" may be put in place but things could well go pretty much the same way in the next speculative fever. Arbitrage is the way to get rich. The question is to what extent can regulation limit excesses (and profits) and so limit social costs (and private losses) when the game is up. A real alternative would require the development of class-based politics to address the systemic corruption of these regimes. External coercion, which would serve good ends, is more difficult, and in any event the motives of outsiders are suspect.

From the IMF perspective, shared by many economists, free capital mobility is a good thing. It makes markets more efficient. Yet prudent regulation is needed, if for no other purpose than that market participants can be supplied with accurate timely information so that their decisions will be well grounded. Even so, the waves of optimism that fuel excess, and the reaction in pessimism and protracted periods of loss of confidence, cannot be prevented. The IMF is needed, in this view, as a lender of last resort to put a bottom under the market to limit the depth and duration of the collapse when swings occur.

The IMF's rescue strategy calls on countries experiencing capital flight to raise domestic interest rates to hold hot money that would otherwise flee the currency. This is done so that the value of the currency does not fall as far as it otherwise would. This is because debts denominated in foreign currencies become impossible to service when the domestic cost of the debt grows from the devaluation. But on the other hand, as we have seen, high interest rates impose a heavy burden on domestic productive capital, which finds the cost of borrowing suddenly beyond its means. The real economy needs credit for the day-to-day business of firms producing goods and services, to finance inventory, and for export credits. Once it is hurt, bankruptcies increase, unemployment grows, and expectations of deepening recession lead to further drops in investment. So there is a conflict between the demand to pay off foreign creditors and the needs of the domestic economy. Countries resist IMF austerity measures, which they believe push their economies into recession-stagnation. The IMF tells them there is no choice.

The Critics

As the IMF has made increasing demands on debtor countries for more basic structural changes in the way their economies operate, especially in the state-corporate relations characteristic of the East Asian developmental model(s), criticism has become more vocal and has originated in surprising places. For example Henry Kissinger, talking to the 1998 Trilateral Commission, said:

> In Southeast Asia, I believe the attempt to solve a currency problem with a huge program of economic reform has created a massive political problem that makes the economic problem insoluble. It means that every economic proposal is seen through the prism of an attempted political revolution by the outside world. Must every last economic institution of the West be transported to other countries? When a country is in trouble, is it really true that globalization requires

that the first thing we tell the country is to devalue its currency and increase
unemployment? Is there no positive message we can bring them, except that in
three years you may be able to go to the market again? [9]

In a similar vein the influential Harvard economist and head of the
National Bureau of Economic Research, Martin Feldstein, has written:
"A nation's desperate need for short-term financial help does not give
the IMF the moral right to substitute its technical judgments for the
outcomes of the nation's political process." [10] Feldstein argues that it is
not the IMF's business to impose structural adjustments not related to
the balance of payments even if such changes would, or might, improve
long-term performance of the economy in question. Robert Wade, a
Brown University political economist, likens the IMF's interventions in
Thailand and Indonesia "to screaming fire in the theater" and "its
intervention in Korea amounted to screaming louder." [11] Jagdish Bhagwati, the prominent Columbia University trade theorist, introduced the
term "Wall St.-Treasury complex," paralleling the military-industrial
complex that President Eisenhower in his farewell address warned was
achieving unwarranted power over the U.S. political economy. What
Bhagwati referred to was a U.S. economic policy based on the thought
that capital's freedom to move in and out of national economies is a
right that the American government must defend as a priority of
international politics. Professor Bhagwati and others questioned
whether Wall Street's interests should come before the right of sovereign
nations to protect their economies from the devastating impact of
short-term capital movements.[12] John Eatwell points to the deflationary
bias of IMF policy measures and the danger they represent for the world
at the end of the twentieth century. [13]

In response to critics, specifically Feldstein, Fisher replied that
macroeconomic adjustment is not the main element of IMF programs in Thailand, Indonesia, and Korea because the heart of their
problem, and so the centerpiece of their programs, is the weakness
of financial institutions, inadequate bank regulation and supervision, and non-transparent relations among corporations, banks, and
the state. The structural and governance issues are key to meaningful
improvement and "markets" insist on real reform or "confidence"
will not return. Therefore, the best course for the IMF is to recapital-

ize or close insolvent banks (let shareholders take their losses but protect small depositors) and take steps to improve regulation and supervision. "Bailout," the IMF insists, is the wrong term for what it does. The IMF lends money. It gets repaid with interest. It does not give away money. In the process it moderates the recession the client country inevitably faces. It gets blamed for the painful adjustment necessary but doesn't overly mind since this shifting of the blame makes it easier for governments to do what needs to be done. The IMF does not seek reelection and so doesn't mind, say fund officials, unofficially.

Stanley Fisher in his response to critics says he does not see why trade liberalization is any less intrusive than banking sector reform. And why not support detailed programs as the fund did in Russia? The IMF, he says, would demand the same in the case of any advanced European country that fell into a similar crisis for similar reasons. It is the fund's job to deal with underlying conditions and to help countries address the structural causes of crises. Countries need to address such fundamental problems if they want fund financial assistance. He stressed the need for macroeconomic balance and a strong and well-supervised financial system as prerequisites for successful liberalization. Indeed, the IMF had been, and continued to pursue an amendment to its charter that would make freeing capital markets an official goal of the organization. The proposed amendment would force total liberalization on unwilling countries and deem continued controls a violation of the (revised) IMF charter. Fisher was quite blunt concerning the control function of the international financial institutions in restructuring national economies.

The IMF Then and Now

In 1944 at the Bretton Woods conference that created the IMF, John Maynard Keynes for the British and Harry Dexter White for the Americans were adamant that liberalization of the capital account was harmful and to be avoided at all cost. It would rob countries of the ability to follow independent economic policies. Importantly Keynes was of the view that markets were irrational. The herd mentality led to bouts of overoptimism. Overextension led to deep pessimism, which also had a tendency to persist too long. Governments had to protect their citizens from runaway animal spirits. As the Keynes plan proclaimed, "it is widely held that control of capital movements, both inward and outward, should be a permanent feature of the post-war economy." The central argument was enshrined in Article VI of the IMF's Articles of Agreement, which endorsed capital controls (and which the IMF now wants to abolish). Echoing Keynes, Martin Wolf has described the recent situation: "The capital markets, when they were euphoric, simply ignored bad news. And when depressed, they have simply ignored the good news. *Either way, they have overshot wildly, and have destabilized the host economies in the process.*" [14]

Markets have been able to destabilize basically healthy East Asian economies because the core countries, primarily the United States supported by Great Britain, have promoted financial market openings that are in the material interests of their financial communities. It is they who have been the greatest beneficiaries of the new global financial regime that undermined the Bretton Woods system. The recipient countries, while profiting from direct foreign investment, which brings with it technological, management, and marketing advantages, are not capital-short economies. They are major savers. They did not need the inflow of speculative capital for national development. It brought asset inflation, which proved to be quite costly. Indeed, those nations, China, Singapore, and Taiwan, that had the largest foreign exchange reserves were able to withstand the speculative threat. In one of history's great ironies the countries that controlled capital flows, from Chile to India, have not been devastated by financial crises. They provide a counter-model for those who now think about imposing restrictions on capital flows. In doing so their experience lends support to the Keynes approach, which the IMF has undermined.

In the 1990s, deregulation of capital markets in Asia allowed massive inflows of short-term capital at a much faster rate than the underlying rate of growth of the economies in question. Despite maintaining favorable macroeconomic fundamentals (growth rates and savings rates were high, inflation low, government deficits under control), they then became vulnerable to destabilizing capital flight when growth slowed down. Kiichi Miyazawa, the former Japanese prime minister, speaking to a 1998 Trilateral Commission gathering in Berlin, summarizing the case along these lines, saw the crisis as demonstrating "the failure of the market. In a nutshell each of these countries failed in their national portfolio management of assets and liabilities."[15] But if the IMF is able to enforce free capital mobility under all conditions at all times, nations can hardly manage such portfolios. They are passive recipients of what markets decide. Miyazawa is not alone in thinking that this is not a healthy situation. The IMF's strategy in the 1980s and 1990s favored transnational finance at the expense of economic stability.

Evaluating the Critiques

Is the problem then that the free market leads to excesses that are socially costly? Yes. Does "crony capitalism" create social costs that made continued growth along state-led lines unsustainable when global conditions change? Yes again. Both explanations are correct. We need not choose between them. Instead we should put both of these explanations in a larger context. It is the development of excess capacity that slows growth and draws capital out of productive spheres and into asset speculation. Since the rich typically have more to say about how their governments function than the rest of us, and this is especially true in countries where military regimes and a lack of democracy prevent workers from organizing unions and citizens from peacefully protesting or contesting in the electoral arena, the way crises develop and are addressed is typically biased in favor of the elites. The most powerful segment of the ruling class is represented by the executive branch of the U.S. government, which functions, as Bhagwati suggests, as a "Wall St.-Treasury complex" favoring globalized finance capital.

If you are willing to grant the validity of such a perspective, then arguments such as whether the IMF should be given more money or not become more complicated. The issue is what will the IMF do with the money? What conditionality will it impose? Is its developmental model one we can endorse fully or in part? This is the question many right-wing Republicans and some left-leaning Democrats were asking. If problems develop because investors take dangerous risks, why should they be protected? The moral hazard problem must again be considered;

if risk is insured people will take still greater risk knowing they will be protected. A lender of last resort would have to have greater regulatory authority to prevent dangerous risk taking. Thus some critics want greater regulation of capital markets. Others suggest that the existence of insurance is the problem. Without insurance private investors and governments would themselves take more care. But what if problems still occur? The debate for the most part is about what if any supranational regulation of financial markets is warranted. The influential Americans in the area of economic policy do not want regulation of markets but rather *regulation of national economic policies by markets*. They believe that market discipline will promote better policies by governments. Most Japanese and other Asians see markets as the problem and want capital mobility regulated. In a basic sense this is a clash between two versions of capitalism: the Anglo-American one with its faith in free markets versus the state-led model that many Asians and others find appealing.

The IMF is not neutral. It is no secret, as Jeffrey Sachs has said that, "the IMF is the instrument by which the U.S. Treasury intervenes in developing countries."[16] In producing bankruptcies through its policies the IMF has reduced the market value of assets dramatically. By forcing banks and other asset holders to sell for what they can get in a buyer's market, the policies favor foreign transnationals with deep pockets. If the IMF packages did not restore confidence in the East Asian economies, they did create conditions propitious to furthering the interests of foreign capital by transforming a short-term liquidity problem into a long-term restructuring crisis. By imposing huge disruptions and deep recession, the IMF is seen by critics as favoring transnational capital, and especially U.S. corporate interests.

If we accept the critical perspective, what then is to be done? First the IMF should cease their demands that all controls on capital mobility be abolished. Second, there should be regulation on short-term capital flow to restore the capacity of countries to better control their own economies. Third, international coordination of policies should provide greater stability and a growth bias and not a deflationary one so that instead of a race to the bottom there could be a leveling upward in the context of growth and shared prosperity. These would be quite substantial changes in direction. We do not discuss them in detail for finance capital and its state allies are not in the market for solutions that put the public safety and well-being ahead of their own interests. The point is that the increased freedom of capital has slowed global growth and can be contrasted to the period after the Second World War during which stable exchange rates supported full employment, progressive taxation, and welfare state programs domestically.

In this chapter we have considered the strongest case, that of the miracle economies of East Asia, to demonstrate the flaws in the international rules urged by the IMF in conjunction with the U.S. Treasury Department, which first force liberalization and then when countries fall victim to financial crisis blame the victims, as if Western financiers and speculative swings had not produced the situations the global economic institutions then take it as their responsibility to address. The IMF saved the banks but imposed harsh conditionality on debtor countries and their people. The story is not fundamentally different in other parts of the world. As Jerome Levinson who is a former general counsel to the Inter-American Bank and former staff director of the U.S. Senate Subcommittee on Multinational Corporations and United States Foreign Policy, has written:

> The theology that has driven this system is an undeviating faith in the unrestricted and unregulated free movement of capital. The objective of U.S. policy has been to assure the security and mobility of that capital. That objective of U.S. policy has overridden all other values or objectives: respect for core worker rights, environmental considerations and an equitable distribution of the burdens of adjustment that have been required to cope with the periodic financial crises afflicting the system. [17]

If the world accepts "the high-risk society" which free capital mobility has ushered in, it will mean rising nationalisms and other movements of resistance as people seek to protect themselves. Some of these movements will be politically destabilizing in reactionary ways. The increased competition for investment will create continued deflationary pressures as countries everywhere attempt to export more at their neighbor's expense. A preferable direction would be to consider reversing the trends that free capital from social controls. In discussing what is to be done, we face the problem of the limits of historical imagination. We have a circumscribed understanding of our elephant. While it appears gargantuan and strong, it in fact has a deep-seated illness. While the doctors minister to it, most of us do our best to avoid injury as it thrashes about. We need a healthy world system to be sure, one that is structured on principles of equality and democratic participation. To create such a system means narrowing the present great inequalities of wealth and power and changing the way decisions are reached. For the people of the Third World and of the core, the clash between local elites and transnational capital frames the political economy debate in a manner that excludes them from any meaningful input into the very decisions that affect their lives.

CHAPTER SIX

Trade Wars, Overinvestment, and Concentration of Capital

The disputes between exporting nations in the age of globalization reopened debate over the nature of trade—who benefits, what rules are appropriate, and how are disagreements to be settled. There is also the question of the larger shape of capitalist development reminiscent of the debates over imperialism at the beginning of the twentieth century, discussed in Chapter Four. In a sense, the same "globalization" issues that seemed uppermost at the start of the twentieth century are again part of the discourse of international political economy at the start of the twenty-first century. Today, rivalries among corporations from different countries get played out in the marketplace and also in disputes between governments seeking advantage for "their" companies. These firms are not only major taxpayers and employers, but also financiers of political campaigns and providers of second careers for elected officials and regulators. They have major political influence. Their activities, which involve alliances on class issues and competition in commercial rivalries, shape history in a host of significant ways.

At the beginning of the twentieth century, some Marxists thought the thrust of capitalist development was to produce an ultra-imperialism in which a new globalized capitalist class would emerge with an interest in avoiding conflict between nations, since it would do business within and among countries. Others saw the uneven expansion of national capitals, and the inevitability that such rivalries could not be peacefully negotiated, and believed that conflict and war were inevitable. At the start of a new century questions of trade wars are again discussed. Many are fearful concerning the possible ramifications of an inability of major trading nations to compromise and settle differences in a harmonious fashion. While there are few predictions of shooting wars among leading trading powers, there is concern that intractable conflicts will reduce willingness to cooperate on new rules for global intercourse.

The more immediate historical parallel is with the late 1920s, when much of the world was already in deep economic crisis. Nations in weak balance-of-payments positions saw exports as their salvation and a round of competitive devaluations and protectionist measures further destabilized the world economy. A major cause of the worldwide war and depression that crippled the first half of the twentieth century was the contention of nations for commodities, raw materials, and markets that produced protectionism and imperial conflict.

Those who worry about trade wars in the present period give central importance to the adoption by the United States of the Smoot-Hawley Tariff and the dramatic decline of world trade as a result of protectionism in the 1930s. Charlene Bershefsky, the U.S. trade representative (in a January 29, 1999, speech), reminded us that for all the contemporary headlines about trade wars and "despite a shock nearly as great as the one that brought the Smoot-Hawley tariff, with 40 percent of the world in recession and six major economies suffering contraction of six percent or more, we as yet see no broad reversion to protectionism." The differences have to do with the growing interpenetration of national economies under the dominance of transnational capital and the hegemonic status of the United States in the world political economy. In the age of globalization, the cost of defending less efficient nation-based corporations becomes more expensive.

The question of whether unrestrained markets unleash forces that can bring on global crisis and world-wide depression seems less abstract than it once did. But even short of any such meltdown, if unrestrained market forces victimize enough people a legitimacy crisis can develop. In the years following the rise of workers' movements in the industrial core, the Bolshevik Revolution, the Great Depression, and the Second

World War, the working class gained greater power while the norm of unrestricted freedom for capital lost legitimacy. Modern liberalism's response to such developments in the postwar period was to foster socially responsible stakeholder capitalism, corporatism, and social democracy, which became important to one degree or another in the advanced economies. The firm's relation to its workers came to be seen in relational terms, as unionized workers were able to command respect as a result of their collective strength. Layoffs of core workers were discouraged and, if deemed necessary, such policies were coupled with interim social insurance and the promise of rehiring when feasible. Productivity-conditioned increases in compensation were considered the norm, at least in the highly organized sectors of the advanced economies. In the Cold War years, class cooperation seemed to many to be an accommodation that paid off for both capital and labor, if not equally. Recovery from the war and the industrialization of previously rural economies (the so-called NICs) intensified competition, and export-oriented development became the dominant model of development. Innovations in communications and transportation allowed economies of scale tied to the high cost of research and development, while brand recognition and the sales effort meant that global presence became increasingly important.

With such developments, transnational capital no longer needed the pretense of social partnership and we witnessed the transformations from a national Keynesian regime of accumulation to one of global neoliberalism. Ironically it was the American oligopolistic industries that first faced the crisis of globalized production. Resultant deindustrialization and restructuring brought erosion to traditional sectors in which organized labor had been strong. In recent decades, deindustrialization and corporate downsizing have been driven by finance capital seeking to impose radical restructuring as a way of sucking surplus by redistributing adjustment costs. The increased importance of the chief financial officer, of the accounting mentality, and of institutional investors was all in part a reaction to a period of rapid inflation from the late 1960s, which the United States unleashed on the world. While this inflationary momentum is a complicated story, it resulted from the oligopolistic structure of postwar U.S. industry with its comfortable cost-plus pricing compounded by efforts to fight the unpopular Vietnam War without raising taxes. The hegemony of the U.S. state allowed America to force adjustment onto others.

These cycles in social structures of accumulation are superimposed on the secular development of capitalism, a process in which all parts of the world have increasingly been brought into a single market with a universalizing of the properties of capitalist social relations. Recalling some of our earlier historical discussion can help clarify the essential features of the role financial orthodoxy played in the misinterpretation of the nature of these developments and in putting forth punishing and finally counterproductive solutions, harmful to the vast majority but in the immediate self-interest of the international financiers. While it is one of our themes that globalization undercuts the sustainability of nationalist economic programs, protectionist forces are still active. On some issues, and for particular industries, they may be of decisive importance.

As transnationals become responsible for more local employment and the future of some national corporations comes to be found in strategic alliances and eventual outright merger with foreign capital, statist politics becomes unsettled in corporatist Europe and among state-led development regimes in the periphery as well. The program of global neoliberalism (which is to open up markets everywhere to competition and penetration by foreign capital) has produced resistance from those whose position is threatened. Inter-capitalist disputes spill into the political arena in many ways, some of which will be discussed in this chapter. Neoliberalism impacts as well on the social possibilities of societies as well. In the latter part of this chapter we shall examine instances in which this has produced tragic consequences.

The contemporary challenge is not the physical conquest of territories directly managed by colonial administrators backed by armies of occupation, but a form of indirect rule through the global state governance institutions, the World Trade Organization, the World Bank, and the International Monetary Fund, which set the rules and guide the local governments, tutoring them in what it is best to do and not to attempt. Yet inter-imperialist rivalries are once again inflaming tensions among major powers. With the Soviet challenge turned back, most of Europe united into a single-currency economic union, Japan more assertive against what it perceives as U.S. bullying, and tensions with other Asian economies, and especially China, over the terms on which the next superpower will be integrated into the global political economy, a multifaceted competition threatens.

For workers these inter-capitalist rivalries would matter less if markets, including labor markets, responded to redeploy resources instantly. Falling prices might not be a problem if people who didn't buy one thing would simply spend the money on other goods and services, creating employment for those released from jobs lost to surging imports or to technological progress. But workers are not pieces of furniture that can be moved around. When overcapacity arises and wages are held down (often by state policies), given the anarchy of production, and the fact that people do not easily move from one industry or type of job to another, serious unemployment as well as overinvestment can arise. Policies that subsidize capital at the expense of collective and individual consumption intensify the sectoral imbalance between ability to produce and capacity to absorb output. The overexpansion of credit for both producers and consumers that helped foster rapid growth becomes a severe problem when growth can no longer be sustained and the ability to service debt diminishes. A decrease of sales or even in the rate of increase in sales is typically the key problem since the asset speculation that buoys the economy is based finally on the performance of the "real" economy. The speculative bubbles that affected Mexico and other Latin American countries and much of East Asia are, as we've seen, phenomena of this sort. Problems may be compounded by the class nature of the states involved, but to blame "crony capitalism" rather than capitalism itself is to misplace causation. Tulip manias and such have a long history suggesting the need for social control of investment rather than continued faith in "efficient" capital markets.

Trade conflicts at the end of the twentieth century ranged from the so-called banana war between the United States and the European Union, to the demand by the American steel industry for protection from unfair foreign competition, to disputes over hormone enhanced beef and genetically modified crops. There is much at stake not only in particular industries (genetically engineered foods and non-food crops are a multi-billion-dollar market), but precedents set on even minor issues (such as bananas) can give long-term advantage to winners. Trade conflicts are high stake battles for those economic interests immediately involved and for the governments backing particular players. The corporations that dominate the global economy, and have corresponding influence over state policies, are overwhelmingly committed to an open trading system that allows them to penetrate smaller markets and overwhelm weaker rivals. The leading states are also engaged in strategic alliances with major competitors based in other countries and continents and see their future in terms of a closely integrated globalized system in which a combination of tactical cooperation and market wars coexist. Trade disputes, while they involve much sound and fury, may as a result be very different from those of the earlier twentieth century because of the emergent oligopolization. Unlike at the beginning of the century when rivalries resulted in the bloody carnage of the First World War, the replay a century or so later is more often farce than tragedy and, in any event, takes place at a different stage of capitalist development. In this chapter we explore national competitiveness in the present era.

Top Banana

One of the most unusual trade disputes was the banana war, given so much play in the late 1990s. It reminded us that much of what is called protectionism has little to do with defending the needs of American and European workers who, after all, do not produce many bananas. The dispute arose because a major donor to the Democratic party wanted to sell more Central American bananas in Europe where preference was given to bananas from Europe's former colonies. The extreme policies of confrontation and possible contagion that both the United States and the Europeans seemed willing to risk appeared totally out of proportion to the stakes involved. But such a rational calculation ignores the new combativeness unleashed by the creation of the European Union's continent-wide market economy and the desire on the part of many European capitalists and politicians to stand up to United States imperialism.

On one side of the banana barricades was Chiquita's Carl Lindner, among the most generous contributors of "soft money"—the balm of instant influence—which made him a legendary presence in Washington politics. (Soft money is that category of unlimited influence that is the elephantine loophole in the ludicrously ineffectual campaign contribution limit law.) On the European side, Lindner's brothers in distributional power also had much to gain, although they talked about protecting the poor and defenseless, the tiny Caribbean islands heavily dependent on banana exports to Europe: St. Vincent, St. Lucia, and Dominica. The Europeans, understanding the American audience, talked darkly about how if these islands lost their banana exporting livelihood they would be forced to become drug transshipment points and worsen the U.S. drug situation.

The European motives were hardly noble. The claim of public-spirited concern for the well-being of the poor and downtrodden does not stand up well. Brent Borrell of the Center for International Economics in Australia and formerly of the World Bank looked carefully at the numbers and found that over half of the money that came from the higher prices Europeans pay for bananas went as surplus profit (or economic rents) to the large distributors who controlled the importation of bananas in Europe, but little to the island producers. He estimated that it cost European consumers $13.25 for every dollar that is received by the producing countries. A 10 percent tax on the market price of bananas sold in Europe and given to the Caribbean islands would help them more and save the European fruit buyers 90 percent of what went to the politically well-connected middlemen. The licensing regime is corrupt and complicated and just might involve substantial soft money transfers to EU political figures.

After losing their case repeatedly through the World Trade Organization dispute resolution mechanism the Europeans responded by slightly changing their rules to meet perhaps the letter, but hardly the spirit of the rulings. The frustrated United States threatened unilateral retaliation in violation of WTO rules and irrevocable damage to the organization through the unleashing of a wider trade war. Both sides acted "deplorably," as the editorial writers say. To maximize the coverage of those who would be made to suffer from 100 percent proposed U.S. tariffs, and presumably to increase as much as possible the interest groups in Europe that will mobilize their influence on behalf of accommodation with America on bananas, the U.S. targeted Belgian chocolates, Scottish cashmere sweaters, French cheeses and designer handbags, Italian Parma hams and other varied and sundry products whose value exceeds $900 million in annual exports to the United States.

Each side engaged in brinkmanship because it wanted to be perceived as so tough that it would have an even better chance of forcing its will in later rounds of trade disputes, an economic strategy paralleling the madman theory of deterrence: we stand ready to blow up the world (or wreck the trade regime) if we do not get our way. Disputes over the export of U.S. hormone-treated beef, which the Europeans do not want to allow into their markets, genetically modified foods, which most Americans accept without question while most Europeans wanted it banned, and a number of other deeply divisive issues crowded the trade agenda. American chemical, pharmaceutical, and agribusiness firms have already flexed their quite considerable muscle on these questions. The popular movements for social justice have been criticized for being "protectionist" when they have shown concern for the economic future of vulnerable working people and their families. There is far less attention to the selfishness and greed of capitalists.

Steel, Increasingly a Less Hardy Perennial

Disputes over steel imports are the sort of conflicts people more traditionally have in mind when they worry about protectionism and trade wars. American steel producers in the late 1990s faced what they saw as a deluge of imports from Japan, Russia, Brazil, and Indonesia, who, it was alleged, were selling steel in the United States below cost. Steel was the focal point, but there were lots of other industries in which excess capacity existed on a global scale. These industries, with high fixed costs, come out ahead selling at a loss so long as revenues covered variable costs. They therefore are likely to export below cost even when this produces protectionist responses and even trade wars. Companies do this all the time within their own economies. It is a competitive response and breaks no law. However, the United States introduced strong anti-dumping laws to prevent foreign producers from selling their goods in U.S. markets if American producers could convince our officials that they were selling below cost. Ironically, anti-dumping legislation, presumably a defense against unfair competition, became a powerful tool of unfair competition to prevent loss of markets in cases when it was the U.S. producers who were uncompetitive. Other countries learned to use anti-dumping laws to protect their producers from competition.

Congress has actively used such anti-dumping procedures to keep out lower cost products from countries that lack the clout to retaliate against the United States. The Clinton White House, on those few occasions when it tried to prevent such measures, was usually frustrated. Few politicians are actually swayed by free trade arguments. They are generally used when convenient and ignored when interests dictate. The interests of the largest, most powerful transnational corporations tend to prevail and "free trade" is enforced against some American companies when larger interests are at stake. The United States, like other countries, is opportunistically a free trader when it serves the purposes of its most powerful economic interests. President Clinton's priorities— his support of NAFTA and his efforts to prevent use of anti-dumping laws to protect lesser capital interests—demonstrated this through the 1990s. For example, the U.S. House of Representatives in March 1999 voted to limit steel imports in violation of WTO rules. A presidential veto was promised should the Senate concur. It was unlikely such limits would again become law, for while the political influence of the industry is substantial, it is not what it once was, and accommodation would be worked out.

Capitalism has changed in many ways in the last century. The once dominant steel sector and the rest of old line industrial America has been eclipsed. The third industrial revolution sectors dependent on information technologies and resurgent finance capital both benefit from and are integral to the mergers that characterize this era and need global markets and an open regulatory architecture. The new leading sectors are not interested in protectionism and indeed are a dominant factor in the American state's effort to enforce a new open international economic order. This does not mean that domestic considerations will not produce nationalistic responses and trade tensions or that the broader costs of globalization will not lead to effective resistance on a broader front and to eventual social regulation.

The United States has done better in the millennial global restructuring, but elsewhere economic stagnation and crisis have had more severe repercussions. The list of offending steel exporters included Japan, which has had a stagnant economy for much of the 1990s after overinvesting in the previous decade and then drowning in excess capacity, and the three large troubled economies, Russia, Indonesia, and Brazil, which, having liberalized capital flows at American insistence, watched their economies being undermined by speculative excesses, unsustainable debt levels, capital flight, dramatic currency depreciation, and economic crisis. These countries, despite U.S. and IMF "rescues," found it difficult or impossible to balance their budgets and pay their debts. They were desperate to export whatever they could at just about any price. They found that the austerity forced upon them by the agents of international finance deepened their domestic recession-cum-depressions and they were not sympathetic to American demands. They believed that American policy demands contributed substantially to the perpetuation of their plight. Japan stood up to the United States on the issue, pointing out that the proposed American action violated World Trade Organization rules, and readied a legal challenge. In a delicate balancing act in which important elements in the Congress continued to reject the idea that the WTO or any other international organization could make binding decisions against U.S. will, it was the executive branch's task to work out deals to avoid open conflict. The executive more forthrightly represents the interests of globalized capital, while congressional representatives are more responsive to local business and labor interests and subject to more traditional populist nationalism.

As in other cases in which trade frictions develop, it is useful to step back from the immediate conflict and ask how these countries got into the messes they were in, and, specifically, how did excess capacity, not only in steel but in everything from hogs to autos, develop and what generated the cycle of speculative lending and default that has produced financial crisis? The questions can be answered in different ways in each particular case: anticipation of perpetual growth of Asian markets (the so-called Pacific century with Asia as the engine of global growth), financial deregulation in the absence of adequate safeguards and ill-conceived loan policies to Brazil and Russia, and crony capitalism (the case that elites ripped off innocent foreign investors and then maximized short-term gain at the expense of long-term stability) are all factors. But whatever the historical variations, such manias, panics, and crises have always been part of the way capitalism works. They are regular occurrences, if unpredictable in terms of exact timing, seriousness, and duration. They arise as part of the uneven nature of capitalist development. Innovation unleashes rapid growth, which produces overinvestment; firms overreach in terms of the expectations they have concerning the future realization of profitable sales and then become unable to service their debt. As overinvestment reaches its peak, speculation in equity and property markets reaches unsustainable proportions, and then these bubbles burst. These cycles involve inflation of asset prices followed by years of painful adjustment. Serious and prolonged downturns have been periods of deflation. This was the case in the Great Depressions of both the end of the nineteenth century and in the 1930s. Steel, the archetypal capital goods industry, suffers particularly from such cycles.

Second, and related to these larger issues, while steel imports rose considerably (they were almost thirty percent of total U.S. consumption in 1997), big steel's more important problem was closer to home, where minimills using newer technologies had captured about half of the steel market and undercut the once powerful industry giants. The steel companies and steel workers who had nowhere else to go had jointly forestalled pollution controls and other regulations in a protracted end game, which they could not in the long run win but since they had no viable exit strategy it was worth just about any cost to forestall further inroads from more competitive sources. The United States lacks the social safety net infrastructure found in many other nations where downsizing cartel arrangements are sponsored by government to reduce unneeded capacity and make losses bearable for participants. Blaming foreign producers is a far more viable strategy than asking assistance for events caused by shifts in technology, although as American trade unionists point out, the help many foreign steel industries and their workers receive from other governments gives them an advantage. This is a matter of degree. The pressures on all are quite similar.

To say that the system in its normal workings shows callous disregard for people is a difficult sell. It forces us to confront the cost of free enterprise. To frame the argument in these terms requires a radical step in popular consciousness. If people begin to think about controlling the ways in which technologies are introduced, looking at how the social costs of their adoption can be minimized and how displaced workers can best be reincorporated productively into the economic order, the discussion moves into new territory. If society accepts that workers are creators of wealth, and so steel workers and not simply the owners of capital are entitled to compensation in any restructurings, the economic calculation becomes a very different one. As simple as this idea is, its acceptance would represents an end to currently existing capitalism.

On another level we can ask about the relationship between excess capacity and the downward pressure on prices that can lead to deflationary crises and deeper contractions. That is, in terms of the stability of the system as it operates, it is important to distinguish between two different types of deflation, one of which imposes another socially costly trajectory. The good kind comes from technological change, which lowers the cost of production so that lower cost increases product demand. Computers are an example. They get cheaper and more efficient over time. This spreads their adoption. Cost declines, but sales go up. The speed of the product cycle in a number of areas has such characteristics. New, cheaper, and better products pour onto a growing market. A second, and very different type of deflation, results from a generalized situation of inadequate demand. Bad deflation results from excess capacity, growing inventories, rising unemployment, falling incomes, and lower consumption cycling downward and possibly resulting in depression. Overcapacity intensifies competition, customers do not respond by buying more, or enough, at the lower price, leading to lower profits, plant closings, and more job loss. As consumer confidence weakens workers, even those who have not lost their jobs grow pessimistic, and companies see no reason to invest in the face of excess capacity and a bleak outlook.

Economies can stagnate, as Japan's did for well over a decade after its bubble economy burst in the late 1980s. For a country, even one as rich as Japan, excess capacity in everything from semiconductors to steel can force producers to lower prices without rekindling growth. Consumers expect still lower prices and are in no hurry to buy. In an aging society retirement worries compound lower present consumption. While all nations try to increase exports, most at the start of the twenty-first century were desperate to do so (the exception was the United States, the consumer of last resort for a world substantially in recession).

More on Historical Parallels

In the second half of the nineteenth century, important innovations in transportation and communication, the railroad and the telegraph, iron-hulled coal-powered ships, and transatlantic cable reduced the cost of doing business over great distances. Developments in metallurgy and chemistry in the latter part of the century produced manufacturing capacity to match the increased extent of the market fueling the imperialist rivalries that led to the First World War. In the interwar period, efforts to reestablish gold parities at prewar levels and to extract reparations from the war's losers and war loans from allies contributed to severe balance-of-payments crises—slow growth, high unemployment, and an inability to address the various imbalances produced by the attempts to return to normalcy—and led to a desire for protection from forces seemingly beyond the control of national policy makers.

The point is that protectionism comes at the end of the story and not at the beginning. To say that trade wars are bad and should be avoided ignores the more crucial matter of the difficulties that create the conditions out of which trade wars become likely, if not inevitable. The end of the First World War found the global economy with excess capacities stimulated by the needs of wartime, a peace which redrew the map of Europe creating new small states that attempted to protect their autonomy, and a situation in which established powers that had experienced differential productivity growth gained or lost economic capacity as a result of war, and disordered exchange rates produced disequilibria that proved difficult to set right. What stability there was in the 1920s depended on a particular balance of international capital flow. When the Fed raised interest rates in the United States this balance was disrupted, confirming the widespread view prevalent over the period since the end of the First World War that the United States neither understood, nor was very interested in, the global financial fragility of the period. The Great Depression can be understood as the outcome of an inability to produce a financial regime capable of sustaining economic growth and stability, the tendency to overinvestment, and to cyclical crises endemic to capitalist development. More market-oriented economists tend to blame government.

I suggest that the same troubling processes are underway in our own time. Today, as in the interwar years, financial orthodoxy is blind to the causes of economic crisis. In large part this is because the class interests it defends tend to benefit from the damage that financial overextension and the consequences of overcapacity have on others. Crisis management reflects historically specific relations between classes domestically and internationally. In this context, the question to be asked is whether United States policies—from the U.S. response to the Latin American debt crisis in the early 1980s to interaction with a new Russian state as it moved away from communism to the East Asian financial crisis beginning in 1997—demonstrated a self-serving stance that did incalculable harm to people in the countries involved, and to the world economy in general. I have made the case that this is, in fact, the proper interpretation, and those concerned with the possibilities of coming trade wars would do well to consider the preconditions in policies demanded by the American Treasury Department on behalf of U.S. financial institutions and enforced by the International Monetary Fund and other agencies. Many of the particular policies in question were the same in the last part of the twentieth century as they were in its early decades.

Orthodoxy argues that free capital markets are automatically efficient. The major difference is that in the earlier period this was presented in terms of the presumed benefits of the gold standard, and even today some analysts look back at the era in which the gold standard regime dominated the as golden age of international finance. They see the failure to properly restore the gold standard after the First World War as responsible for the Great Depression. But, as we have argued, the damage done in efforts to restore the gold standard, and the pressure on exchange rates and production costs it exacerbates, was the principal threat to financial stability and economic prosperity between the wars. It was a large part of the problem and not the solution. Adherence to the gold standard forced contractionary policies, which turned recession into depression.

The gold standard was part of an ideological stance toward laissez-faire capitalism, which was hegemonic. Its ideological bias was to insist that any government interference with market forces was bound to do more harm than good. As a result nations were held back from taking actions that might have averted or reduced the impact of crisis. The political power of finance led to economic outcomes favored by bankers but harmful to societies at large. The same may be said of the current period. The self-interested actions of national governments and the false belief in the gold standard's automaticity led to failure to reach agreement on the need for, and the specifics of, central bank cooperation. There were powerful voices—one thinks first of John Maynard Keynes—who warned of the dangers. But then as now, orthodoxy was strong. Allegiance to the belief in the harmonious nature of free capital markets and the sanctity of debt contracts prevails until the cost of economic crisis grows to the point that even the most obtuse must consider governmental action.

After the Great Depression and the carnage of the Second World War, a conflict which owed so much to the inability of Germany to recover during the interwar years, the result in significant measure of the demand for reparations that perpetuated economic suffering in Germany and paved the way for Hitler, it was widely understood that avoiding a replay when peace was restored would involve a very different international financial regime. The globalization of finance from the 1970s, like the effort to reimpose the international gold standard or gold exchange standard in the interwar years, constrained national policy makers and led to the demand for protectionism.

The tension between free capital movements and free trade was well understood by the architects of the post–Second World War Bretton Woods regime who saw free trade, economic growth, and full employment as dependent on the control of capital. It was recognized in the 1940s and 1950s that abolishing exchange controls would make it exceedingly difficult, if not impossible, for any government that might come to power to pursue full employment and welfare state redistributive policies without provoking capital flight. Industrial capital, which dominated in the early postwar years, understood this and, sold on the need for Keynesian policies, favored continued capital controls. As the financial sector recovered and multinational corporations came to hold a more globalist view, the establishment in the United States moved toward unanimity in favor of free capital mobility. England, looking to its future as a financial center, supported the Americans in this resolve. In the 1940s, bankers arguing along these lines made the case that a more open financial order would prevent governments from meddling with market forces. They were overruled by industrial capital, which saw merit in the Keynesian stimulus that was understood to need some degree of capital control to be effective. With growing internationalization, policy changes followed that favored greater freedom for international speculators.

The United States and Britain, by creating the Euromarket, undermined the Bretton Woods system unilaterally, offering mobile financial traders the ability to increasingly operate without regulation and so forcing other financial centers to liberalize markets or see their business and capital migrate. This process of competitive deregulation parallels in its impact the competitive devaluation policies of the 1930s. It was the political choice most significantly in the irresponsibility of the United States in the 1960s in unleashing inflation and making others bear its cost, and then unilaterally changing the rules at the expense of foreign central banks and others who believed the U.S. commitment to its fixed exchange rate, and also the opportunist choice of Great Britain to pursue a deregulation strategy that would solidify its position as a global financial center.

In 1972 foreign direct investment from the United States was six times the amount of FDI into the United States. We were investing much more abroad than foreigners were investing here in production facilities and other tangible wealth-producing investments. The United States was also exporting less in relation to imports. In 1971 the United States ran its first merchandise deficit since 1893. It was in that year that the United States formally devalued the dollar to address this loss of competitiveness, a loss not so much of U.S. transnational competitiveness, but of production capacity at home. The lower dollar made U.S. products cost less for foreigners in their now stronger currencies and also reduced the cost for United States–based transnational corporations selling here but producing abroad.

The weakening dollar in the 1970s and dramatically rising inflation led to hardliner Paul Volcker's appointment as chair of the Federal Reserve. He dramatically restricted the growth of the money supply. Interest rates and unemployment shot up. By 1982, the unemployment rate reached a level that had not been seen since the Great Depression. President Reagan signaled, with his firing of the air traffic controllers, whose union ironically had been one of the few to support his presidential bid, an anti-labor offensive, which forced down the real wages of American workers and produced a climate in the 1990s in which employment could rise but real wages would not. (Real wages are wages adjusted for changes in the price level and in taxation.)

The high real-interest rates acted as a magnet drawing funds from all over the world, which financed the tripling of the national debt under President Reagan. Ironically, Reagan called for a balanced budget amendment to the U.S. Constitution to restrain "tax and spend" Democrats from raising taxes. But Reagan himself produced a huge structural deficit with his tax cuts for the corporate rich and dramatic increases in military spending. It was funded by foreign borrowing and paid down with cuts in social spending. The tax and spend strategy of the Reagan administration was, as Reagan's budget director David Stockman frankly confessed, a Trojan horse to win the victory over the welfare state, which the Reagan people could not attack directly due to its popularity. By creating such a huge structural deficit with tax cuts (almost all of which went to the upper fifth of the income distribution and within that exclusive company overwhelmingly to the richest one-half of one percent of all Americans) he was able to force dramatic cuts in programs that helped the working class and the lowest income Americans. In the early years of the twenty-first century, President George W. Bush was able to recycle these policies and ideas.

The Contemporary Situation

In the 1990s these forces became even stronger under new Democrat Bill Clinton and new Labour under the leadership of Tony Blair, both of whom favored policies of financial openness and a deregulated international monetary regime. Clinton's ability to win the decisive backing of Democratic party donors among Wall Street investment bankers was crucial to his bid for the presidency. Under the Clinton administration there was a stepping up of long-established priorities. Clinton's Commerce Department was under the leadership of Ron Brown who was continuously on the road pushing American exports and demanding financial market liberalization. Clinton created the National Economic Council as a counterpart to the National Security Council, and Robert Rubin, its head, guided the global ideological shift to unrestricted financial flows, to the great profit of financial service firms such as Rubin's old firm Goldman, Sachs. Asia was a particular target for this full court press as we have seen. Continued access to U.S. markets was held hostage to liberalization of financial markets. Korea, for example, was sponsored by the United States for membership in the OECD, the Organization for Cooperation and Development, the rich nations club, in exchange for accelerated liberalization of its financial markets. The Koreans let their companies borrow abroad even though such loans might make their corporations vulnerable to a panic-driven outflow, which did occur at the end of 1997. The cost of the business won by American banks and brokerage firms was paid by the Asian economies. As treasury secretary, Rubin and his assistant, and later successor, Lawrence Summers, pressed the International Monetary Fund to amend its charter to make free capital movements a central goal for the IMF in its negotiations with member countries when they came for balance-of-payments assistance.

The leaders of Asia, Latin America, and even continental Europe have increasingly articulated the view that recent financial crises have been caused by unregulated cross-border financial trading. Financial liberalization, in the words of Mahathir Mohamed, Malaysia's prime minister, has driven the forces that resulted in the demise of the East Asian miracle. "The great Asian Tigers are no more. Reduced to whimpering and begging, they are but a former shadow of themselves.... From being miracle economies we have now become impoverished nations." Percival Patterson, prime minister of Jamaica, is not alone in blaming the way the IMF handled the crisis. "As a lender of last resort, the IMF remains unsuited to that role. . . . Within its limited resources, it did bail out the creditors, which leaves the debtors in the lurch." Resentment at American policies and the gains the United States has reaped from its own and from IMF policies led increasingly to a backlash against the U.S. model, which serves Wall Street speculators while sacrificing the people of the Third World. The larger context continues to echo the early decades of the twentieth century when similar policies of orthodoxy benefiting finance capital at the expense of global economic growth and stability were dominant. The United States appears to be replicating the conditions and policies that produced the Great Depression. This does not mean that history will be repeated, or repeated in the same way, but that the earlier patterns and the power of orthodoxy have returned, and are as destructive as ever.

It has been argued that when things began to crumble, the United States and the International Monetary Fund demanded policies that made conditions worse. The austerity demanded, the high interest rates, and the continued currency convertibility enabled foreign investors to get their funds out while locals in the affected countries bore the disproportionate burden of the devastating adjustments that followed. Throughout Indonesia, Korea, and elsewhere, small-business owners lost their businesses, workers lost their jobs, and foreign banks were rewarded with sharply higher interest rates and government guarantees against default, at taxpayer expense. As Milton Friedman commented, "The United States does give foreign aid. But it is a different kind of foreign aid. It only goes through countries like Thailand to Bankers Trust."

With the remarkable performance of the U.S. economy compared to that of the rest of the world, Rubin retired in 1999, enjoying a reputation as one of the best treasury secretaries the United States has had. Internationally, he is widely criticized as being responsible for encouraging policies that have produced instability and economic crisis and by forcing financial liberalization. Representing the United States, he stood virtually alone (his only significant support coming from the British) in opposing efforts to curb the volatility of capital markets. It is also widely understood that the money centers of Wall Street and its counterpart the City in London have profited substantially from this turmoil.

The Europeans, Japanese, and Third World countries that favored some form of international agreement on new modes of managing international financial markets have been unable to budge the United States or to successfully oppose its will. The self-serving American policies of "the Wall Street-Treasury-IMF complex" have come in for near universal criticism outside of Anglo-American financial policy maker circles. George W. Bush's administration, influenced by such free market thinking, looked to the harsh medicines of market deregulation over liberal institutionalist social engineering. Even in the absence of a wider melt-down it should be evident that it was the forced liberalization of financial markets that led to the crises in not only Asia, but Russia and Latin America, and produced huge U.S. trade deficits provoking protectionist demands. But it would be a mistake to expect trade wars to develop out of this as in the first half of the twentieth century.

The Threat of Protectionism?

Transnational corporations are responsible for three-quarters of world trade in manufactured goods. Over a third of that is trade among affiliates of the same company. This makes it somewhat misplaced for nationalists to worry about "foreign" competition and blame the workers in other countries for taking "our" jobs. It is "our" corporations that have organized the new pattern of globalized production. For the United States such intrafirm trade was about 60 percent of the total of all merchandise traded at the start of the 1990s. Protectionism isn't what it used to be because transnationals want to keep importing goods from production sites abroad that they either directly own or indirectly control through long-term relational contracting.

When the transnational corporations lose in Congress, which is more responsive to local constituencies and so to job loss as a result of trade policies, they go to the executive branch. Whether the incumbent president is a Democrat or a Republican, the executive is far more responsive to their interests. Since the executive branch is in charge of interpreting and enforcing the laws this often proves a successful strategy. For example when Congress passed "Made in America" labeling, the transnational corporations lobbied the Federal Trade Commission to interpret "Made in America" to mean that, among other things, running shoes made in China could be labeled "Made in America." The FTC agreed to relax standards to accommodate transnational corporate interests. However, a ferocious counter-campaign from consumer and labor groups inundated Washington with angry postcards and physical presence. The *New York Times* reported, "What started out as an effort to recognize the reality of American commerce in the global bazaar had unexpectedly turned into an often-times emotional referendum on product quality, truth in labeling, the power of unions and old-fashioned patriotism." [1]

The regulators, used to talking to industry lobbyists and not to voter-taxpayer citizens, tried to explain that it was a "complicated issue." They did not see that they had made a mistake in going along with the industry proposal to emasculate the intent of the "Made In America" labeling law. "What we have here," said one Washington insider who had thought it was a done deal, "is a failure to communicate." [2] Similar maneuvering goes on in other countries as those most deeply imbricated in the globalized economy lobby their governments to see matters their way and abandon the long-time nationalistic stance still supported by most citizens.

Globalization and Economic Restructuring

The growing importance of finance as a tool of economic restructuring is one of our constant themes. Another is the use of state power to favor the interests of transnational capital and finance. Into the late 1990s a strong dollar drew capital to American financial markets and funded consumption and investment in this country and also provided the funding for United States–based finance capital and transnational corporations to buy up productive assets in other parts of the world. It is this growing power of the most internationalized sections of capital that is the subtext of globalization.

The world's economies are now so interpenetrated by transnational control that Korea's or Japan's problems are more likely to lead to the takeover of their large but weakened corporate giants by U.S. capital than to trade wars between nationalist capitalist classes. The extent of foreign ownership is substantial. Foreign-owned enterprises in France (which we think of as so nationalistic, for example) account for 25 percent of industrial production. Forty percent of the United Kingdom's exports are by foreign firms. By the late 1980s the flow of foreign direct investment into the United States was exceeding the outflow. Strategies of promoting national champions have given way to strategic alliances and outright mergers with foreign rivals to increase market power and to offset the huge research and development costs of designing new products and marketing them on a global scale. By the early 1990s the top twenty-five multinational corporations all had sales over $25 billion. The largest (in 1992), General Motors, had sales larger than the gross domestic product of all but twenty-one nations. Lists of countries by GDP and companies by sales showed Toyota's sales exceeding the GDP of Portugal and Poland, IBM larger than Venezuela, and Unilever exceeding New Zealand. The growth of transnational corporations and the importance of direct foreign investment means that such firms operate in a very large number of countries and have a high proportion of their assets, workers, and profits from locations beyond their home countries. Trade wars become counterproductive for the dominant economic actors in the globalized economy.

By the start of the twenty-first century the dominant U.S. corporations, if measured by stock market valuation rather than by corporate sales figures, were the high-tech leaders like Microsoft, transnational marketers, most prominently Wal-Mart, and financial giants led by Citigroup. Indeed, looked at by market valuation, General Motors was far down the list, well below such upstart newcomers as AOL, Oracle, Dell, Yahoo!, and Sun Microsystems. Increasingly the danger is not old-style trade wars but the greater dominance of these corporate giants over the economic lives of working people everywhere. When oligopolistic structure is concentrated a relatively small number of giants come to dominate world markets, controlling information and money flows.

In concert with state agencies, these giants exercise power over culture and finance to political as well as narrowly economic advantage.

There is growing awareness, as Jeffrey Garten, dean of the Yale School of Management, and former Clinton administration official writes, that "Megacompanies are almost beyond the law." They have the money to run legal circles around regulators and to intimidate smaller rivals. They can buy political influence both with campaign contributions and by threatening job loss among electorates in jurisdictions in which labor, environmental, or tax law is not to their liking. They can demand subsidies and shift social costs to workers and governments.

This is not to say that there will not be demands for protectionism and even the adoption of protectionist policies. But such protectionism is likely to be exercised by the strong who are able to get away with its unilateral exercise of discriminatory policies. To see why this is the case, consider the example of steel once again. In early 1998, agreement was reached between the Clinton administration and Russia to strictly control the growth of its steel exports to the United States. Russia cut back to the level of sales before the sharp fall in the value of the ruble. That the Russians agreed to this when steel exports were such a huge source of scarce hard currency is a measure of the leverage the United States has over Russia. It does not really matter that the World Trade Organization rules forbid this kind of managed trade agreement or voluntary export restraint. Russia is not a member of the WTO. But if the United States had not forced such an agreement from the Russians, it could have levied a steep tariff on its steel exports and thus could have stopped them. Russia, which is negotiating for more aid from the International Monetary Fund, knows that Robert Rubin has been integrally involved in those negotiations. They are in no position to anger the United States. Brazil was also unlikely to retaliate against the Commerce Department's decision to impose huge tariffs on their hot-rolled steel sent to the United States.

If, as the balance of trade continued to widen, unemployment rose in the United States, we would likely see more demands for protection by workers fearing job loss and companies with their backs to the wall will blame unfair foreign competition. Such nationalist appeals will receive a sympathetic hearing, especially if they are from a large, well-organized industry able to flex political muscle. Yet the power of transnational capital puts a cap on what even well-organized domestic interests can expect as isolated bargainers in the new world order. However, the framing of the issue this way is both incomplete and misleading. If old-style flexing of political muscle by "special interests" is less effective, class awareness has been developing and so has a backlash against corporate power. Whether this will translate into a move from traditional special interest protectionism to a wider demand for protection against the destabilization caused by economic shifts remains to be seen. Freedom of capital without social regulation unleashes painful costs as governments, workers, and weaker competitors are forced into a deflation that orthodox policy makers and the financial interests that have such influence over their direction dictate that the interests of speculative capital come before the needs of ordinary people and the stability of economies. There is nothing new in this, and today as in the past, the cost the world pays for such policies is inordinately high and may grow more severe.

The flashpoint for a possible trade war of a dimension that could be truly destabilizing is between the United States and the European Union, because only the EU is capable of standing up to the United States's economic, military, and political capacities, and even there, divisions within the European Union are an important factor in determining the extent to which it would oppose the pressures of the United States. Some countries are much closer to American policy makers than others. England, whether under Conservative or Labour governments, is a close ally. This is in part for historical reasons, but it is also because in the U.K. finance capital is the dominant economic force and an open financial order is in its interest as well as that of the United States–based global financial giants. Continental Europeans, France and Germany particularly, see the threat of financial liberalization and are in the vanguard of resisting the offensive of Anglo-American financiers backed by their respective governments.

The simplified theorization of the state evident in the early twentieth-century imperialism literature and in the equally economistic and reductionist theories of the state in the 1970s, which saw an unproblematic structural or instrumental state as the captive of some entity called capital, did not allow for a more subtle political analysis of the way different state formations and fractions of capital, popular movements, and partisan positioning influence international political economy. Any revised use of an imperialist analysis will need a more sophisticated theory of the state, of political contestations, and of the formation and alliance building of class fractions in the real world rather than ideal type historical conjunctures. This is especially important as we consider political strategies for progressive moments in the twenty-first century.

Pre-Keynesian Orthodoxy

As we have seen, in matters of trade as for issues of finance after the hiatus of the postwar era in which national Keynesianism dominated we have returned to earlier orthodoxies. The national Keynesian model was born of recognition that unregulated market capitalism was dangerous. The Great Depression and its costs were all too obvious to a postwar generation intent on using government to stimulate equitable growth. National Keynesianism had different forms in different places. In Latin America populist regimes pursued import substitution industrialization under a political alliance in which industrial elites needed the support of urban workers against the ruling landed oligarchies. In Western Europe capitalism had been discredited by the collapse of the 1920s and 1930s and capitalists in many countries discredited by their collaboration with fascist regimes. Labor and the left came out of the war with high prestige and organized strength so that social democratic corporatist governance structures developed out of the material needs and the constellation of class forces. National champions were protected and subsidized. Capital controls retained. In Japan and later other nations of East Asia, a corporatism without labor emerged under more authoritarian political conditions to pursue state-led development.

This postwar era came to an end for reasons we have discussed earlier. Transnational corporations, first United States–based multinationals and then those of other countries, international banks, and other large financial institutions, sought freedom to invest and worked to undermine statist restrictions. Developments lowering the cost of information processing and transfer assisted in this task. Telecom and asset management innovations continued to push these developments forward. The material interests of these leading transnational firms were advanced by the international financial institutions, which used economic crises unleashed by destabilizing capital movements into and out of national economies to advance the interests of transnational capital. In doing so they reprised pre-Keynesian orthodoxies. This became clear when we compared their prescriptions with those of the interwar years.

We also saw how with the end of the Cold War transnational capital revised its "state theory" and practice. The brutal dictatorships that characterized the "free world" regimes of the periphery, with their naked repression, mass murders, torture, and extortionist attitudes toward business activity within their territories, are, in the new climate, for the most part no longer the preferred form of governance. They are costly, inefficient from a business point of view, and tend to crystallize mass opposition, which they can repress only at significant cost and at the risk of promoting mass movements that take on anti-capitalist ideologies (since repression and foreign capitalist control are widely understood as linked). Better to have democratic governments managed by local elites tied to transnational capital's globalist vision. That way it is well-meaning democratically elected governments that enforce IMF austerity, making the point that "there is no alternative" to market-oriented globalism. A local business class ruling through elections is a better partner for transnational capital, once the threat of revolution recedes, than a more obvious repressive rent-seeking military regime.

The insistence on the trappings of formal democracy, regular elections, and a relatively free press does not threaten unwelcome change. Modern media-intensive elections have come to most parts of the world. They are expensive. Freedom of the press extends to those who are rich enough to own the press and the TV stations. Capital dominates the electoral process. Once the threat of revolution is removed by the tightened constraints of international finance, repressive tolerance can emerge. There is less radical resistance under its rule than under more overtly imperious governments. It is harder to resist consumer society's seductions. Formal equality before the law diminishes the moral outrage grossly repressive regimes generate. But most of all it is the neoliberal trade and finance regime that constrains national autonomy, limiting what is expected of governments. Repression of dissent and exploitation of workers becomes less obvious, and perhaps more effective.

Growth and Opportunity Neo-Colonial Style

In the 1990s a variety of initiatives were undertaken by transnational capital through the agency of the US state to impose a new constitutionalism on the world community. From NAFTA, the North American Free Trade Agreement, to the proposed MAI, the Multilateral Agreement on Investment, governments were asked to commit themselves to allow capital the right to freely invest anywhere and in any sectors of the local economy it wanted, and to roll back existing restrictions on capital.

One such effort to force neoliberal restructuring was introduced in 1998 by Philip Crane, a Republican from Illinois. His "Africa Growth and Opportunity Act" was passed by the U.S. House of Representatives and Richard Lugar, a Republican from Indiana, introduced a similar measure in the Senate. In May 2000, President Clinton signed the bill into law as Title 1 of the U.S. Trade and Development Act. Its purpose was described as promoting democratization and good government by tying economic benefits to economic reforms. The act required African nations to protect property rights, guarantee foreign property against expropriation, reduce "high" import and corporate taxes, and demanded that African governments spend less and minimize their interventions in the market through such measures as price controls and subsidies. Aid would be conditional on the degree of market-friendly reforms.

African countries would only get favorable access to U.S. markets if they abide by conditions similar to those of the NAFTA, which favors foreign investors in a number of important particulars, and specifically requires budget cuts and in other ways the Washington consensus. Those who favor the bill accuse its opponents of heartless cruelty. They particularly point out that the African continent is being ravaged by AIDS, that 290 million Africans, more than the entire population of the

United States, live on the equivalent of a dollar a day or less, and that "little Honduras" now exports seven times more textiles to the U.S. than all the nations of sub-Saharan Africa. The problem, according to Thomas Friedman, the *New York Times* columnist and resident expert on globalization, is "the AFL-CIO crowd." He writes, "Shame on them, after all the unions' phony-baloney assertions in Seattle that they just want to improve workers' rights around the world and help the poor." To say that the bill gives trade concessions to Africa and that only selfish, protectionist U.S. trade unions oppose it seriously misrepresents the facts.

Representative Jesse Jackson, Jr., called the legislation the "Africa Recolonization Act" and said, "Contempt for African economic self-determination defines this legislation—a posture most clearly exemplified by the act's declaration that not one shred of its so-called benefits shall be conferred upon any African nation until the nation submits to U.S. imposed terms for how it shall run its economic, legal and social systems. We treat no other region in the world in this fashion." It is not clear that he is right on the last point. It is U.S. policy to impose such conditionality on all countries. The trade press, for example, called the bill "NAFTA for Africa." [3]

The reason he spoke of the act's "so-called" benefits is that many of the provisions were written by U.S. corporations and are not guided by the needs of Africa. For example, among its requirements, African textiles were to contain U.S. thread and the fabric to be spun and cut in the U.S. if textiles were to be eligible for the bill's benefits. The interim bill had another textile provision that would allow Chinese-made apparel and textiles to be considered "African," even if Africans did no work, so long as they are transhipped through Africa. Given the constitution of power within the Congress it was, sadly, a foregone conclusion which approach would become law.

As a number of critics pointed out, the prime beneficiaries of the plan are American corporations. The bill required the sale of natural resources, cuts in corporate taxes, and domestic spending to pay foreign debts. Its benefits for Africa are minimal and mostly enumerate benefits the administration could provide without new legislation if it wanted. As Congressman Jackson says, "Missing from the bill is any mention of the four items that all African nations and African policy advocates agree are the basis for sovereign and sustainable development: Debt relief, sovereignty to choose economic and social policy, fair trade and investment rules, and aid to overcome the damage done by rich countries through their past exploitation of the continent." Jackson proposed an alternative bill that would have respected African sovereignty and stressed sustainable development and debt cancellation. An alternative to the current IMF-US policy would require massive activism and rebuilding of the anti-imperialist movement. Deeper criticism would face the collusion of many of the regions' governments in the exploitation of their people and the extent to which local elites have benefited from the suffering of their own people. The class nature of African societies would be a part of such a deeper analysis.

Not only would we want to investigate who put the dictators in power and armed them over the decades of so-called independence and years of Cold War "ends justify the means" policy, but look more closely at how the bankers' priorities and the greed of transnationals such as the pharmaceutical companies have conditioned African development. Sub-Saharan Africa had negative growth rates in the lost decade of the 1980s and when the figures for the 1990s are in there is unlikely to be improvement. Earlier I mentioned the way one pundit invokes the horrors of the African AIDS crisis to browbeat opponents of the bogus "Africa Growth and Opportunity Act," as if opposing this bad piece of legislation would prolong the epidemic. It is worth pursuing this subject to make a very different point. The AIDS crisis is indeed grave. At the start of the twenty-first century, one in eight South Africans was HIV-positive (70 percent or so of the world's victims of HIV and AIDS are in sub-Saharan Africa). South Africa has already suffered a million AIDS deaths, nearly double the number of people who have died in the United States.

The standard drug therapies used in the West cost more than $12,000 a year at market prices. The average annual income in South Africa is less than three thousand dollars and the country has one of the most unequal income distributions in the world, a legacy of apartheid. In 1997, faced with the AIDS situation the South African government began a program of compulsory licensing (which compelled drug companies to authorize local manufacturers to produce a generic version that can save up to 90 percent) and parallel importation (importing them from countries where they are available at more reasonable prices than those charged by the American pharmaceutical companies). The government went abroad and bought in bulk. The foreign, predominantly U.S., drug companies say that they would not have spent money developing these drugs unless they could sell them at what they consider reasonable profits to cover the cost and risk of development. In fact, the AIDS drugs were developed with tax dollars and then marketing rights were assigned to private firms.

Forty major companies jointly filed suit in South Africa's Constitutional Court. In fact however TRIP (the Trade Related Intellectual Property Rights Agreement of the WTO) allows both parallel importing and compulsory licensing by countries faced with a national emergency. The U.S. Congress, ever ready to do the bidding of large U.S.-based transnational corporations, cut off foreign aid to South Africa in an effort to pressure it on behalf of these companies. According to a report to Congress from the office of the U.S. trade Representative (February 5, 1999), "All relevant agencies of the U.S. government . . . have been engaged in an assiduous, concerted campaign" to get South Africa to capitulate. Commerce Secretary William Daley pushed the South African government to capitulate. The United States tried to kill a World Health Organization resolution urging members to "ensure that public health interests are paramount in pharmaceutical and health policies."[4]

The big drug companies had been very generous to the Washington insiders. Demonstrators showed up repeatedly when Vice President Gore spoke publicly with signs and leaflets explaining that these pharmaceutical companies had paid the Clinton–Gore folks well over half a million dollars and that Gore was playing an active role in pressuring the South African government on behalf of the drugmakers. Stories began to appear in the mainstream press with details of the vice president's and his key advisers' close connections to the industry. As a result of this activist pressure Gore finally capitulated and wrote a letter to James Clyburn, the chairman of the Congressional Black Caucus, saying that he supported South Africa's efforts to provide AIDS drugs through parallel importing and compulsory licensing "so long as they are carried out in a way that is consistent with international agreements," the last a face-saving device since South Africa had repeatedly given assurances that it would do just that. The drug industry, also under substantial public attack, announced it had suspended its suit. In the two years of the American campaign an estimated 300,000 South Africans had died of AIDS. The issue of course was not settled in a way that would permanently make affordable drugs available to people living with AIDS in South Africa.

The movement for social justice kept the pressure on. It has begun as well to make broader connections. Indeed, it has expanded its campaign to cover prevention and treatment of other diseases that disproportionately attack the poor, like malaria which cost Africa up to $100 billion in gross domestic product over the last three decades and continues to slow growth dramatically. Malaria kills between one and two million people a year, 90 percent of them Africans. The issue again is closely tied to the debt crisis. Debt in this instance too is killing people. As Jeffrey Sachs, the Harvard development economist, reported in early 2000, "This year, Nigeria will spend five times its public health budget on debt servicing. I will argue that the right thing would be to ask the government to come up with a program including AIDS and malaria control in exchange for debt forgiveness." [5] The benefits from effective malaria control alone could translate to between $3 billion and $12 billion a year in higher GDP (and of course save lives). The goal is achievable, but there would need to be a different attitude and commitment from the centers of finance capital.

The global movement for social justice is raising such issues and making connections that reflect the widespread and growing awareness of the meanings of the interdependence of the international political economy. With globalization has come in many ways a redefinition of property rights, entitlements, and responsibilities. For the most part, as the era of national Keynesianism faded and the period of neoliberal dominance advanced, it has been capital that has dominated this process. At the start of the twenty-first century the social movements have gained greater influence in response to the widespread perception that new rules for the world political economy are needed and that the regimes produced by the global state economic governance institutions do not provide the socially responsible frame required. In this chapter we have seen that even in the seemingly abstruse area of trade policy the meanings and significance of "protectionism" and "protection" need to be carefully examined for their social and political significance. The failure to develop effective safeguards for livelihoods and an unwillingness to share on an equitable basis the potential benefits of science and industry have produced a world of growing inequality and an absolute increase in poverty, which in a rational social order would not be necessary and for many people is no longer acceptable.

The damage done by falling commodity prices, massive debt repayment, and the legacies of colonialism have received increasing notice because of the dire poverty and the deteriorating situation in Africa. In other parts of the world where economic indicators look better, especially where U.S. investors are doing well, there is less attention to the consequences of structural adjustment demands. In Latin America the continued effects go beyond those of the "lost decade" of the 1980s during which macro indicators were so dismal. The profit recovery of the 1990s has been at the expense of the masses of the region. Carlos Vilas has described how the concept of the legal working week, one of the first achievements of the Latin American labor movement, has nearly disappeared:

> The state has played a strategic role in the reconfiguration of the labor market. Latin American governments have enacted regressive labor-law reforms, substituted commercial law for labor law, shown permissiveness in the face of company violations of labor laws and eased labor regulations in order to allow companies to hire, alter working conditions, and fire personnel virtually at will. The privatization of social security, cutbacks in public spending on education, health, and recreation, and the privatization of these services, all have heightened the vulnerability of the working class. . . . Social legislation that had its origins in the principle of the compensation of workers for their vulnerability vis-à-vis capital have been replaced by a principle of abstract equality which legitimates and reinforces the supremacy of capital over labor.[6]

New rules are being promoted in a host of guises. The extent, meaning, and even existence of these attempts to produce a new set of rules for capital's domination of the global economy are not sufficiently understood by most Americans. This does not mean, however, that average citizens do not have strongly held opinions on the morality of such free market principles and practices, nor that important protests are not occurring. The sense of the basic unfairness of corporate rule and the dangers of its policies from genetically modified food to its control over the media and power to buy elected officials as well as its exploitation of working people and control over their lives and life space are all matters that cannot help but produce continuous tensions and resistance. Class struggle, pronounced a relic of the past, becomes transformed in its social and cultural forms in the new economy. Those who expect the end of history are living out the fantasies ruling-class ideology has always embraced. The forms of organized resistance change as labor and human rights, environmental protection, and protection of community mobilize a new generation into anti-systemic movements that in our own time as in the past will rock the power structure and in time may overcome it.

The questions raised with regard to making AIDS and malaria drugs available for those who would otherwise die, the obvious gains in a social cost/social benefit sense of increasing investment not simply in health care and disease prevention, but in education, mass transportation, and local community development suggest that taking some goods and services from the arena of provision only for those who can pay and seeing them as social goods with demonstrably large positive externalities that need to be societal priorities may be redefining the line between the private and the public, moving it back toward the public. This process involves a redefinition of property rights and the responsibilities of the world community to its members, which could create a version of welfare state provision for an era of globalization. The demand for radical changes in what we think of as private and best left to the profit motive and where social needs must trump private profit criteria is the driving force of the emergent movement for global social justice. In the last two chapters we turn more explicitly to the struggle to define globalization-globality and international solidarity in the coming decades.

CHAPTER SEVEN

Globalization and the Assault on U.S. Citizenship

Globalization, Labor, and Citizenship

The U.S. state and large corporations based in the United States clearly play the lead role in setting the rules of the global economy. In this context, it might seem logical to argue that because the United States is the major beneficiary of globalization, the Americans protesting against globalization, while they may be concerned with broader, human-rights issues, are actually acting against their own best interests. There is some truth in this view, and it is among the achievements of the anti-globalization campaign that it has enabled increasing numbers of people to think about political issues from the perspective of international solidarity rather than narrow self-interest. But this conception is also misleading, insofar as globalization is also an assault on citizenship rights not only in the Third World and the former Soviet bloc, but in the United States itself. The process not only creates and reinforces relations of inequality and domination on a global scale, but also affects, on a smaller scale, every society involved in the process. The global domination of U.S. corporate interests requires increasingly oppressive forms of domination within the United States as well. This is most apparent in the changing conditions of labor. And as a heavier burden is placed on labor, so U.S. citizenship rights are eroded more broadly.

At the level of pure theory, when trade increases between a rich country and a poor one it is the lower wage earners, the less educated workers in a rich country, who lose out and capital, the abundant factor in the rich country, that gains. Yet the pure theory of international trade is less relevant to the real world as the assumptions on which it is based become outdated. For example, the theory assumes that although goods are traded between countries, factors of production—including labor and capital—do not move across borders. But in today's world, transnational corporations move their capital and technology around the world while controlling brand-name marketing. They bring production to labor even as migration both legal and undocumented restructures the labor markets of the core. The treatment of workers is a political matter and not merely a reflection of the marginal productivity of labor.

The most free market–oriented economies, the United States and the UK, have experienced the greatest extent and most rapid increase in inequality. In continental Europe social protections help low-wage workers, and all workers on average do better in such countries than they do in the Anglo-American ones. It is also not clear, though it is frequently said, that European social democracies pay a high price for these social protections in slower growth and higher unemployment. But the celebrated U.S. lead in productivity and lower unemployment in the late 1990s is not evident over the longer period of the entire business cycle. Further, the 1999 OECD annual employment outlook shows that there is no clear link between employment protection laws and an expansion of temporary jobs. Instead, tight regulation ensures more stable jobs, less labor turnover, and fewer unemployed. Europe's slower growth and austerity, resulting from policies required by the Maastricht Treaty, which established the criteria for joining the euro, have had the greatest hand in raising unemployment. Actually, productivity is higher per worker in Europe and unemployment for prime-age males not so different if we count the millions of (predominantly black) men in prison in the United States as unemployed. They just get a different "benefit" package than the one supplied by social democratic welfare states to their jobless workers.

In the United States during the recent period of accelerated globalization, we have seen the expansion of a set of arrangements that have forced dramatically longer hours, a rapid growth in part-time jobs, and more family members joining the work force in an effort to raise living standards in the face of stagnant or falling real wages. This has made the United States as an economic entity more competitive. The benefits of the improvement have been at the expense of most working people who have lost out. U.S. workers are forced to accept a downward push in living standards, insufficient provision for retirement or health care, and lack of vacation time or other benefits so that on a global level, the United States can "stay competitive." William Cline of the Institute for International Economies finds that 39 percent of the increase in wage inequality over the last twenty years has been the result of international trade patterns.[1] In this sense, U.S. domination of the process of capitalist globalization has inflicted its cost not only on the rest of the world but on most Americans as well.

At the same time millionaires and billionaires have benefited most from growing inequality. While in most advanced economies top corporate executives earn an average of six to ten or even twenty times what their workers do, in the United States the remuneration of an average chief executive of a big U.S. company was 475 times greater than that of the average non-managerial worker, according to a survey done for *Business Week* (more than six times the difference a decade earlier). Just as the conditions of labor have been made more arduous in order to advance their interests, so the dominant ideological patterns and political alignments have been redefined in this cause.

Rolling Back the Forty-Hour Week

Adjusting for the dramatic increase in hours per year in the U.S., Americans now work more hours than anyone else, including the Japanese. Real wages (adjusting for changes in the price level) have stagnated even as labor costs have dropped significantly. Until the mid-1990s real wages had lagged for over twenty years. Even as productivity grew real wages did not. Of the increase in working-class income in the latter years of the 1990s, only half came from families earning more income per hour worked. The other half came from employees putting in more hours.

The real median wage in the United States at the end of the 1990s, as we noted in Chapter One, was no higher than it was in 1973. Real wages at the bottom were actually close to 10 percent lower, even though per capita income had risen by 70 percent. More workers—10 percent of the labor force—were temporary workers or "independent contractors." At Microsoft alone there are 6,000 such people. A third of the temps had been with the company a year or more. Such people are known as "permatemps." They are hired by Microsoft managers and then asked to sign up with a temp agency. They do the same work but without the same benefits. Such practices are being challenged in a unionization drive and in the courts. This second-class citizenship group is growing. Roughly a third of the salaried part-time employees surveyed in the 1997 National Study of the Changing Work Force said they spent at least thirty-five hours on the job. The government doesn't know how many "full-time part-timers" there are, but there is general consensus that in the new risk economy part-time work is a full-time problem for many. [2]

Full-time work has also become a problem as forced overtime has become mandatory for more and more employees. A strike by telephone workers against Verizon in the summer of 2000 was motivated in large part by overtime issues; women in the company's calling centers complained that they could not break free from work early enough to pick up their children or make dinner for their families. Firefighters in Connecticut challenged the constitutionality of mandatory overtime, arguing, unsuccessfully as it turned out, that it violated the Thirteenth Amendment ban on slavery. Management classifies increasing numbers of its employees as "managers" so that they can ignore hour limitations entirely, forcing employees to take work home and do it on their own time in a legal twilight zone of coerced and unpaid overtime on a fixed salary that routinely demands over sixty-hour weeks. Such people increasingly conceive of themselves as workers and are receptive to organizing in professional unions and associations. Here, too, we are back a century or more. In 1886 the eight-hour movement (and the Haymarket police riot in Chicago) spurred activity that fifty-two years later finally resulted in the forty-hour workweek with the passage of the Fair Labor Standards Act in 1938. Today this law is a joke for millions of Americans and work fatigue has once again become a labor issue of wide importance. [3]

Until things were changed by the Great Depression and the popular movement that brought about the New Deal, economists argued that governments shouldn't pass laws to limit hours or impose safe working conditions as these interfered with the freedom of individuals to enter contracts on whatever terms they wished. If women and children agreed to work twelve-hour days in the textile mills, if men lost their lives in unsafe mines, what was this to government? The ideology of deregulation has become the dominant ethos roughly from the time of Ronald Reagan's presidency, making it easier to chip away at health and safety protection and the real value of the minimum wage. As America depended on the magic of the marketplace, poverty and inequality grew to become the worst among the advanced economies, taking us back in many ways to the situation at the beginning of the twentieth century when elite organizations also worked to co-opt public leaders and misrepresent social reality through the media and the political parties they controlled.

Technology that replaces labor is not in and of itself objectionable. Machines that lighten human labor are desirable—if workers thereby gain a higher standard of living. But where workers are merely cast aside and, because of age, lack of training, or other causes, lose their livelihood or are forced into worse employment choices, the system profits at the expense of those who create the wealth. Globalization is only one factor in this equation. Most jobs are lost for a "good" reason. We can all have a higher standard of living when technology allows replacing human labor and multiplies the contribution each worker can make. More agricultural or manufacturing output with fewer workers required is a fine thing *if those displaced move to equally or more highly compensated and more satisfying work.* It is a question of how the gains are shared or not shared and the extent to which one group of people bears a costly burden. If change is better for society as a whole, it creates a surplus, which in theory is available to pay the adjustment cost for those adversely affected in significant ways. It is the failure of societies to address such issues of social justice that have been central to movements opposing "free" trade and technological "progress."

However dramatic the images of globalization's impacts and its realities in terms of plants closing here and opening in the Third World may be, most manufacturing jobs are lost as the result of labor-displacing technology. When Dwight Eisenhower was president of the United States in the 1950s, 35 percent of all workers were in manufacturing. At the end of the twentieth century the figure was less than 18 percent while manufacturing production had tripled. More is produced with fewer workers. The major problem for American workers is not simply the import of products from the Third World (the United States also exports and exports have been a major source of job growth), but rather the bargaining context, the legislative and legal frame that produces low wages, loss of benefits, growth of contingent work, involuntary part-time work, lack of secure job tenure, increasing use of temps who do the same work but for less pay with no benefits, and non-enforcement of minimum wage and hours of work legislation. We, the "we" who respond from a working-class perspective on these issues, need to expand our understanding of globalization to explore how labor has lost out politically, how this impacts us economically, and what can be done. That Americans work in offices more than in factories is not in and of itself a bad thing. The transition from our being almost exclusively an agricultural nation in 1776 to an industrial giant two centuries later made for a higher standard of living. By the latter date, 1 or 2 percent of the work force could feed the nation (and contribute substantially to export earnings), leaving most Americans the opportunity to produce additional goods and services. Technology does have a revolutionary capacity to raise living standards. The issue is how the technology is directed and how its potential benefits are distributed.

It is well to remember that while jobs are destroyed, employment is created in new industries. Expansion in media, business services, telecom, finance, software, and information processing have been important sources of job creation in America. These are major export industries. Their growth has contributed to the low unemployment rate in the United States at the start of the new millennium. But it is also well to bear in mind that the culture of these industries is different than old-style basic industry. Forms of labor control and the extent and distribution of benefits are different. These sectors are not unionized.

Even in industries with rapidly increasing demand for unskilled and semiskilled labor, wages are low, job security problematic. In the United States at the start of the twenty-first century, hourly real wages for production workers are no higher than they were in the 1970s after adjusting for inflation and regressive changes in taxation. Income and wealth inequalities increased. The rising stock market did not bring capital gains to the majority of working people. They owned no stock.

This is not just affecting factory workers and low-wage service workers. The Dilberts of the world also see their work lives as alienated, their relation to their employers as involving exploitation. We may note, for example, as one indicator that from the mid-1980s to the mid-1990s work spaces (increasingly cell-like cubicles, or desks cheek by jowl) shrunk by 25 to 50 percent for the employees at seventy big trend-setting companies, according to the Facility Performance Group, which keeps track of such things.[4] More jobs are part-time and offer fewer benefits than old-style unionized employment did. The new economy is not as kind to working people as the management "worker empowerment" interpretation of new technologies suggests. As noted, the higher salaries and wages of some workers in the early twenty-first century came not so much from higher pay but longer hours worked. The cell phone, pager, e-mail, and fax allowed a 24/7 work life in which private time was eroded by the ability of communications innovations to keep more and more people in the work loop no matter where they are or what time of day or night it is. Work time expands with the information revolution.

Redefining Consumer Sovereignty

The new technology now also allows a fundamental shift in how we are treated as customers. In the new business model, marketers use masses of data to create a customer profiles, in an almost Orwellian sense. "For the first time, companies can truly measure exactly what such service costs on an individual level and assess the return on each dollar. They can know exactly how much business someone generates, what he is likely to buy, and how much it cost to answer the phone. That allows them to deliver a level of service based on each person's potential to produce a profit—and not a single phone-call more."

"The result," Diane Brody writes, "could be a whole new stratification of consumer society. The top tier may enjoy an unprecedented level of personal attention. But those who fall below a certain level of profitability for too long may find themselves bounced from the customer rolls altogether or facing fees that all but usher them out the door."[5] The dramatic fall in the costs of processing information allows banks to identify incoming phone calls from customers, to classify these calls by priority from most valued to least valued, putting the former at the head of the line to receive customized service, the latter on perpetual hold to encourage them to move their business elsewhere. Similarly banks can use information to cross-sell financial and other service products such as insurance and mutual funds with greater confidence gleaned by what they know about their customers' finances. Some companies produce profit and loss statements for each of their customers, allowing them to zero in on the ones they want. [6] From here it is a small step to link financial records, to health information and employment history. Your interview with school psychologists, and a list of the 900 numbers you may have called, are all in data bases that can be accessed and merged. Acxiom Corporation in Conway, Arkansas, claims to have combined public and consumer information on 95 percent of American households.

Information technology gives companies the ability to discriminate against customers and potential customers who will not bring them adequate profits. The top tier will be pampered even more. The rest will be given menu choices and will spend hours pressing one for this and seven for that, frustrated and unable to complain because the company doesn't care about them. The service divide adds a new dimension to class inequality. The recorded message tells us our business is important to them. The reality is that accumulation goes better with dehumanization of not only work but consumption as well. The low-profit customer is no longer entitled to much of anything from such information technology–driven systems. You don't know when you're being directed to a different telephone queue and you never hear about the benefits you're missing. You don't realize that your power to negotiate with everyone from gate agents to bank employees is predetermined by the code next to your name on a computer screen. If service "stinks," as Brody puts it, this is part of a deliberate profit strategy.

We may all be able to use the new technology to conveniently bank at home (and save money doing so for our financial institutions), but top customers see a web icon that directs them to a live service agent for a phone conversation. The rest of us never see it. In one example of how the new information technology stratifies, a bank "codes its credit-card customers with tiny colored squares that flash when service reps call up an account on their computer screens. Green means a person is a profitable customer and should be granted waivers or otherwise given white-glove treatment. Reds are the money-losers who have almost no negotiating power, and yellow is a more discretionary category in between." [7]

Not only do the poor pay more. The rich pay less and get better deals. The best advice to counter being put on hold while your betters are pampered is to avoid releasing your personal information. The less they know about you the less they can slot you. Don't punch in those numbers if you are a low-value customer—and welcome to the new world of customer apartheid. Information and communication technologies also allow a blurring of the boundaries between work and consumption. Ursula Hews offers the example of an order for an airline ticket "may be transmitted over the telephone and keyed in by a call-center worker or entered directly on the airline's website by the customer; the labor of data entry might be either paid or unpaid." Customers do more and more of the work for companies whether it is searching for flights online or punching numbers on their telephone in response to recorded menus because companies have automated some "service," putting the work onto the customer. [8]

The Internet-related technologies suggest the possibilities of an even greater Orwellian mind control by totalitarian governance structures. There is more reason to be concerned about higher and more insidious forms of control by capital. The phrase "invasion of privacy" does not begin to capture the uses to which the new database information economy is being put and potentially can be put to use. The Internetted economy raises new issues, and many old and familiar ones, in a new context. Technology is not neutral.

AOL Time Warner can gather, does gather, information on individuals' tastes in books, records, and the sites they visit to buy clothes, travel services, and pornography. All of these can all be tracked and correlated with medical records, social security numbers, driving records, and hobbies, the consumers delivered in matched sets to advertisers interested in targeting particular potential customers. Combined with credit card records not only can particular products be pitched, but insurance companies could potentially screen out people who have been to websites indicating possible costly illnesses. Employers could profile potential and actual employees to screen out ones they do not want. The AOL Time Warner merger is not simply about stock prices and who will make how much money, although it is about this things surely, but it is also about who will more broadly shape our economy and society in the twenty-first century.

In July 1997, AOL sold subscriber phone numbers to telemarketers, reversing the policy only after a major public uproar made the cost of the backlash greater than the potential profit to be made. Even after one tells AOL not to send online promotions the company forces members to make the request again or face new promotions. Less high profile companies do far more. Doubleclick, a company that tracks consumers around the web by inserting "cookies" onto their computers without asking permission, correlates online habits with huge databases and then sells them to advertisers who can personally attack consumers in areas of susceptibility. Their sales pitches are able to track along to sites visited by individual users. They can see what you might be looking to buy and then hit you with ads for competing products. In early 2000, Doubleclick had about 100 million such detailed profiles. While Doubleclick promises not to collect data on sexual behavior, finance and medical, or children's surfing habits, its promise is not legally binding. Doubleclick, whose stock went up by more than a thousand percent in 1999, says a majority of consumers want targeted ads. It also makes it nearly impossible to opt out and most people don't even know it is tracking their every step on the Internet. Other competitors use similar tactics. Recently the *Wall Street Journal* carried a four-page advertising spread by a company called Digital Archaeology explaining what their software could do. "There's Janet. The last time she ordered parrot food she also browsed dog care tips." "Spends at least $120 every time she shops online, but only $85 when purchasing by catalog." "Responds to your direct mail, not your television spots." It remains to be seen whether consumer activists will succeed in bringing such practices under social regulation. As things stand, you could look up medical insurance online and then be barraged by unsolicited e-mails from insurance companies.

The government in the United States does little to interfere with such "free enterprise." The Federal Trade Commission, for example, under public pressure, promises it will analyze the stated policies of such companies—but not their actual behavior. Many companies routinely violate their announced policies. The California HealthCare Foundation, for example, studied companies that promised to keep medical records private, finding that all but three of the nineteen sites they sampled violated their own stated practices. Industry self-regulation is the American way and there are organizations that certify privacy practices. None of these self-policing industry groups has ever pulled its seal of approval from members who pay for the false protection consumers believe they derive from such industry tools. The technology allows, among other things, advertisers to pick up any personal information a customer enters on a web page displaying a banner advertisement without the provider of the page or the user's knowing. Since these common banner ads are sold by third parties, the company whose website it is can promise privacy as their own policy and this becomes a meaningless promise even if one presumes the best of intentions.

As we move online to buy and to bank who is going to guarantee the value of cyber currencies? What if your bank disappears from its website? Or you have differences with a service provider who turns out to be incorporated in Nigeria or Paraguay? In Europe, where the concern for privacy and protection is at a much higher level than in the United States (here protecting children from pornography seems the only concern taken seriously by Congress), there are government data police already limiting corporate snooping. People must opt-in. That is, advertisers need user permission to compile data on them. People can refuse. They can insist that information only be used for the immediate purpose agreed upon and nothing else. U.S. corporations are challenging such "anti-competitive" practices. European privacy policies and the policing of privacy codes are much more advanced. This raises questions of how the sort of harmonization by federal legislation of varying state policies in the United States of a hundred years ago will be paralleled in an era of globalization and national sovereignty.

The importance of the struggle over the definition of rights should not be underestimated. Information policy involves issues of property rights and class struggle. Patent laws seem arcane but they define what digital information can be owned and who can access it under what conditions. There are questions of legal identity online. What is binding and how is legal capacity to be determined and verified. In all of these issues there are intra-corporate disputes as they try to carve up how much of us different capitals will control. These are issues of how people can defend themselves in their personas as workers and consumers from the far-reaching control of information capitals.

We cannot know the balance between the liberatory potential of new technologies and their capacity to produce new forms of social control, and even a new feudalism in which workers are watched through their PCs, their e-mail accessed and their voice mail monitored. A 1997 survey by the American Management Association of 900 large corporations found that nearly two-thirds of them admit some form of electronic surveillance of their own workers.[9] Resisting such invasion of privacy and the commodification of personal identity is difficult because governments support the expansion of commerce and are funded by the new giants who shape our lives. Government is thus caught between popular outrage and its support of major economic players. Moreover the state itself is under attack by these transnational giants as they jockey for new markets. The attack on the public provision of goods and services is a major case in point and takes many forms. While governments privatized service delivery, when they have been considered slow in doing so, corporations have shown little hesitancy to prompt them. In 1994 United Parcel Service, a U.S. company, took the European Union executive to European court for failure to investigate its charges that the German post office was subsidizing its money-losing parcel service, which competed with UPS.

The Ideology of Globalization

Much has been written on the ideological power of globalization as a construct of inevitability. Edward Luttwak, for example, writes: "Elite

Americans do not merely approve of globalization. They treasure it as their common ideology, almost a religion." [10] This is not to say that the process of globalization depends on winning ideological consent alone. Economic coercion is an inextricable part of the process. This was well illustrated within weeks of the Seattle WTO Ministerial Meetings when *Business Week* ran a story of how General Electric suppliers were being pushed, indeed forced on pain of losing their contracts, to close down plants in the United States and set up in Mexico. GE even puts on "supplier migration" conferences to press the point. The message is clearly presented: "Migrate or be out of business; not a matter of if, just when. This is not a seminar just to provide information. We expect you to move and move quickly," is the quote the magazine offers from a corporate internal report. [11] GE is one of the world's largest corporations. It is highly profitable. That such a firm would be "squeezing the lemons," in one of the favorite phrases of its long-time CEO, Jack Welch, the lemons being its workers and suppliers, in this way seemed unfair to many. But investors were more inclined to agree with those media pundits who dismiss critics by reminding them, "That's capitalism. That is the way the system works." The ideology of globalization serves to legitimate this and also more direct and brutal forms of coercion.

Economists make essentially the same claims they have been making for centuries and yet most people are not convinced. They stress job creation, lower cost, production, and efficiency. Critics argue that the gain of lower-priced goods does not make up for the dislocations and suffering imposed on the people whose lives are destabilized by these developments. The victims of globalization, and those who fear they may become its victims, are a constituency for radical movements of all types since their mainstream elected officials and opinion makers deny the legitimacy of their complaints, or assert that protested changes are inevitable, unavoidable, and good for the society. Economists talk in terms of the general interest, of total gains exceeding any costs involved. From a class perspective we may ask: If globalization is so good, why do some groups pay while others get so very much out of it? Why is poverty being reproduced so extensively, why are inequalities so great? Why are working people less secure? Why are they so vulnerable if they are supposed to be better off? A clearer account of the ideology of globalization can help to clarify these questions.

In the late 1990s, the three-quarters of the American population without university degrees were getting paid on average 20 percent less when they found new jobs after being laid off, according to Department of Labor studies. Lack of quality public education is an important factor in growing income inequality in the United States. Unlike in the United States, in countries like France, Germany, and the Netherlands the supply of educated workers has grown rapidly, preventing the growth of wage differentials. A comparison between the United States and Canada supports the argument that it may not be the rise of new technology that is crucial but government's failure to improve education in a climate of weak unions and lack of support for working-class living standards through government-provided health care and other aspects of the social wage. The gainers, the better educated and upper income groups who have the good jobs and who hold the overwhelming claim to ownership of capital, have received almost all of the benefits. The average income of the richest one percent of Americans, adjusted for tax and inflation, rose by about 90 percent between 1986 and 1997. Over these years 90 percent of Americans saw their average spending power go up by 1.6 percent. This made the idea of a tax cut popular among many working people who had seen their incomes stagnate.

But the income tax cuts promised and those delivered by politicians have made their lives more difficult, not easier. This is because (in the latest year available at this writing, 1997) only about 6 percent of taxpayers earned $100,000 or more. But this group paid over half of all income taxes collected that year. A tax cut provides more income to this small, wealthy group and is paid for out of service cuts, money that could have gone into education and health care for all. The social security taxes—the major tax paid by working people—keep rising. These are regressive taxes, and the $100,000 and over group pay a lower proportion of their income in social security taxes than a worker earning the minimum wage. When politicians speak about "letting you spend your own money," they are cynically currying favor for policies that give to the richest and take from the majority of the

American people. The corporations and the affluent are the "we" of informed public opinion and the force behind the media molding of public opinion. Of course $100,000—even if it is more than 94 percent of the taxpayers earned in 1997—is not the real money. It is the millionaires and billionaires who have benefited most from growing inequality.

While few Americans can recite the statistics on tax burden and growing income inequality there is a general awareness of the way things have been going. Perhaps the most interesting post-Seattle commentary was the Harris Poll, which confirmed what other surveys have shown. Most Americans (52 percent in the poll) were sympathetic to the concerns of the demonstrators. "Echoing the anti-business themes that ran through the sound bites and across the banners there, the BW-Harris poll also found that most Americans believe that business now has too much power." And while *Business Week* claimed it as "a puzzling anomaly" that in the greatest period of wealth creation in U.S. history so many people could be "living in another era," it also quoted a Princeton economist who pointed out that in the real world, people are still living from paycheck to paycheck and that "the tremendous wealth creation has by and large gone to the people at the top."[12] Most of the demonstrators, as the establishment press well understood, had the sort of class analysis that working people intuitively, if inchoately, often have, and they were tired of being told that globalization was good and to just shut up.

The movements for social justice who sponsored the Seattle protests reject the nationalist responses favored by Pat Buchanan and Ross Perot as morally repugnant and not terribly relevant to an era of globalization. This is, after all, a world in which, as John Ruggie has written, "IBM is Japan's largest computer exporter, and Sony is the largest exporter of television sets from the United States. It is the world in which Brother Industries, a Japanese concern assembling typewriters in Bartlett, Tennessee, brings an antidumping case before the U.S. International Trade Commission against Smith Corona, an American firm that imports typewriters into the United States from its offshore facilities in Singapore and Indonesia."[13] To think in terms of U.S. corporations versus foreign corporations, of "our" capitalists versus "their" capitalists, is anachronistic. To think in terms of a nation-alism in which all Americans, owners and workers, should stand to-gether to protect an "us" against "them" is foolishness, and should be understood as such by working-class Americans. The corporations that fight it out for supremacy are trying to increase their returns to stockholders. The goals and concerns of the firms are not necessarily those a democratic politics would choose to guide how the larger society is to operate.

The Corporate Masters of U.S. Politics

Support of globalization was strong in the high-income brackets while among the majority of American families, those with incomes under $50,000, the positive view of globalization was held by just 37 percent. Such views are based on experience. As Kate Bronfenbrenner has shown in careful studies of the threat of runaway plants on unioni-zation efforts and workers' ability to make demands for better wages and working conditions, globalization in the form of plant closing threats and actual plant closings are extremely pervasive and effective components of employers' anti-labor strategy. From 1993 to 1995 em-ployers threatened to close plants in half of all certification elections and often made good on the threats. The 15 percent shutdown rate within two years of certification election victories was triple the rate found by researchers in the late 1980s before NAFTA (the North American Free Trade Agreement) went into effect. By the late 1990s, two-thirds of U.S. companies in manufacturing and communica-tions were threatening to relocate all or part of their operations when faced with attempts by U.S. workers to form a union. This contrasted sharply with the late 1980s, when less than 30 percent of employers made similar threats.[14] No wonder the majority of Americans have doubts about free trade. Most believe U.S. trade policy pays too much attention to the concerns of the transnational corporations and too little to those of working Americans.[15] It is clear that the demonstrators had wide support of their fellow citizens.

Globally more than a third of international trade is within global production units. More than half the exports of foreign affiliates of United States and Japanese firms go to other parts of the same company's production network and about 40 percent of parent firm exports go to their foreign affiliates, according to United Nations data.[16] With such economic power comes political power. As Michael Zweig has written:

> Trade is not the problem. The problem is trade without standards to block the effects of greed. Capitalists of course want the greatest freedom they can win for themselves. They tend to think they are entitled to go anywhere and do anything that makes a profit. Their demand to be able to invest internationally without restriction just expands their demand to be freed from burdensome labor and environmental restrictions in the United States. The same motive, to get rich by any means available, at any cost to others, drives them at home and abroad. [17]

While almost all Americans appreciate the benefits of international trade, support for free trade is overwhelmingly an elite phenomenon. Polls consistently show a majority saying cheaper imports hurt wages and that therefore trade should be managed. They understand that exports create jobs and that lower cost imports help consumers. But for most people the question is how trade effects their livelihood. Most Americans would pay more to help preserve living standards of workers. They would like the better jobs and higher pay that trade theory promises, but they are rightly skeptical. They would also pay more for imports in order to change working conditions for those workers in low-wage countries who they see routinely exploited by United States–based transnationals. Americans and others are not against trade but rather the rules of trade that capital has imposed, which are widely viewed as unfair.

The dissatisfaction with practices of national politics, is now blamed on globalization, predates the awareness of the phenomenon. It has to do with the way money rules all aspects of social life including the electoral one. Economic inequalities condition the way campaigns are financed and the manner in which economic inequality in democratic states pollutes democratic practice and sets the terms of policy making. If we had a society in which auto workers and nurses had as much of a voice as corporate PR representatives and lawyer-lobbyists have now, we would have a very different type of governance discourse and, as a result, a completely different approach to how to deal with globalization. If we had a level playing field for participation and influence, globalization would be less a synonym for imperialism and mean something more like global solidarity.

Trade heightens awareness of class issues. There is growing clarity that global capital can be regulated to produce in ways that are less harmful to labor and the environment. Indeed, just as workers within countries found that if they could organize all workers in an industry they would be in a strong position in negotiating with employers, so international solidarity strengthens all. The global economy is just the capitalist system operating across national boundaries. As it has gotten easier for capital to organize production in complex cross-border patterns of supply and manufacturing, it becomes essential that workers who in fact have social relations with each other make an effort to unite. Those who face a common employer, even if this is obscured by the fetishism of the commodities they jointly produce and the cash nexus that binds them together, need to understand their connected fates.

The Silicon Coalition, which has emerged in early twenty-first-century America, is not so different from the Morgan corporate interests of a century before. History books record the corruption of the political and regulatory processes of an earlier era, but we see that these business strategies are not without their contemporary counterparts. At the start of the twenty-first century the new Democrats in Congress compete with free market Republicans to support high-tech business and to court campaign contributions, which, these new industry leaders have learned, are necessary to grease the wheels of progress, suggesting that "geek megabucks" were funding a "virtual third party" and turning the relation "into good ol' pork barrel politics."[18]

As the Justice Department brought its case against Microsoft, Bill Gates hired lobbying firms to attempt to get Congress to reduce the funding of the antitrust division of the Justice Department. When its efforts came to light, Mr. Gates claimed that all Microsoft was doing was to speak out against PR funding going to the antitrust division. The propriety of such an attack on the government by the largest corporation in America was not helped by the fact that the antitrust division did not have a PR budget. It had one spokeswoman assigned to it by the Justice Department's central office of public affairs. In fact, Microsoft had tried to arrange a $9 million cut from the Justice Department's modest $114 million budget request. The *Washington Post* suggested it was rather unusual for a firm "to seek an across-the-board cut in a department's budget, especially in the middle of a major court battle" and Thomas Friedman, summarizing the affair in a *New York Times* column, asked, "What happens to democracies when companies grow to size extra-extra-large, in order to compete globally, but democratic regulatory institutions—like the antitrust division of the Justice Department—remain a size small?" It was time, he suggested, that "instead of just being dazzled by these mega-mergers, there should be a nagging voice in us all asking: Is democracy going to be bought up too?" [19]

Indeed when the contemporary Rockefeller, Bill Gates, facing a court ruling that his company repeatedly violated antitrust law, came to Washington, he was treated like a rock star, according to the press. House Republicans asked him to up Microsoft's contributions to GOP candidates. Senate Majority Leader Trent Lott suggested investigation of overzealous prosecution of Microsoft. Just two days after a federal judge denounced Microsoft as a predatory monopolist President Clinton is photographed with his arms around Gates's shoulders praising his charitable contributions, perhaps conveying a message to the Justice Department's antitrust officials.[20]

Matters at the start of the twenty-first century were not all that different from those of a century earlier. Early capitalists resisted child labor laws, unions, and social control generally. They were certainly not thrilled at the demands for antitrust regulation and progressive and more effective corporate taxation at a national level. Yet all of these major changes occurred in the advanced economies. In the twenty-first century they should take place on a global scale. The same conservative forces that said these changes should not be allowed to happen at the domestic level now talk of the unspeakable harm social regulation of capital at a global level will bring. There is no more reason to listen to them now than there was a century ago. To say that the global village needs a set of rules by which all will abide does not mean these have to be the rules preferred by transnational capital, or that favor one set of capitalists over another and for both to gain at the expense of workers and the environment. The issue is how best to build movements to bring about the most sensible and effective rules, from the point of view of the world's working people.

CHAPTER EIGHT

Progressive Globalism: Challenging the Audacity of Capital

This discussion of globalization has for the most part been a critical one. The argument has not been to end international exchange or preclude the building of a better world community, but rather to recognize the need to set equitable rules for the global political economy. The dramatic development of the forces of production and potential new technologies are important for raising living standards. The achievements of the human imagination and the realization of new ways to make lives better and more interesting are, however, scarred by the form commodification so often takes, which constrains rather than emancipates.

It is the social relations under which these breakthroughs are controlled, their subservience to the goal of accumulation, and their negative impacts on the lives of working people and the planet that have been stressed in contrast to the usual celebratory voices of mainstream commentators. The instabilities and harmful social and ecological consequences that accompany this process required more attention than the mainstream's upbeat presentation admits. The issue is not whether we are one world, but what kind of world we shall have, what values will be uppermost, and whether working people and the environment must be sacrificed to a growth mentality that is silent about the costs its trajectory imposes.

Since the end of the postwar period, the international financial institutions, most importantly the IMF, have focused on neoliberal goals to erode the political force of national Keynesianism, social democracy, and socialism. New financial institutions reflect this changed emphasis. For example, price stability is the European Central Bank's sole mandate with not even the rhetorical support for growth and employment that is assigned the Federal Reserve by law in the United States. The euro, the Maastricht convergence criteria, and attempts at international institution reformation such as the proposed Multilateral Agreement on Investment are all premised on the logic of freedom for capital at the expense of social priorities. International governance becomes the conduit for the greater dominance of finance capital. That there has been massive social protest under these conditions is hardly a surprise.

The class recomposition of recent decades has reinforced these developments. In what has been called the Third World, local elites no longer pursue protectionist national development strategies but welcome openness and their role as regional agents of international capital. They work to integrate their economies into globalized networks, typically not seeking the best deal for their country's workers and taxpayers. In the advanced countries too the growth of information-communications sectors tied to the globalization process changes the consciousness of many technical professional workers and others. Better-paid workers who saw their job prospects improve and their retirement nest eggs grow in mutual fund portfolios have a significant material interest in speculative investments tied to rapid restructuring. The banks and financiers prefer a redistributive growth in which subsidies flow from working-class tax payers who are geographically less mobile toward capital that has substantial mobility and demands incentives to locate or to stay put. The growing power of financial markets thus has serious consequences—a drop in effective taxation of capital and of the rich, whose wealth is mobile, to falling real wages for working people and lower social welfare spending. Governments everywhere found themselves under pressure to finance their expenditures from working-class regressive sources and to cut borrowing and the level of spending by severe financial market pressures.

The pressure of financial markets to raise returns leads to pressure for short-term gains, downsizing, and the selling off of lower than average profit-making units. The number of direct employees of Fortune 500 companies has declined precipitously as a result of relentless pruning, contracting out, and greater use of part-time and other contingent employees. Returns to owners have been enhanced by the abrogation of implicit and even written contracts, asset stripping, and the use of debt in place of equity. The growing use of stock options has made the single-minded pursuit of profit for owners coincide with incentives for top executives. The pressure on corporate executives who tried to defend their traditional prerogatives came from institutional investors, corporate raiders, and restructuring buy-out advisers. Companies that do not aggressively maximize shareholder value have been taken over by those willing to throw out the old managers and downsize the work force. The momentum has been relentless and hardly limited to restoring past profit margins. It has been about maximizing returns to owners regardless of the impact on workers and communities.

The world economy at the start of the new millennium depended on a peculiar and unsustainable mathematics of capital flows. The top tier of U.S. consumers spent lavishly, to a significant measure because of the wealth effect of rising equity prices. Working-class consumers went deeper into debt. Spending exceeded income, an unsustainable pattern. The growing U.S. trade deficit was equivalent to 3 percent of GDP at the start of the twenty-first century. Global excess capacity meant bargains for shoppers and money pouring into financial markets seeking secure returns. As income grew more unequal and the wealth of the top 10 percent and especially of the super-rich 1 percent soared, money was funneled into stock-market investments often using significant leverage to maximize the amounts put at risk and increasing the supply of funds competing for equities fueling stock-market expansion, a situation that reminds many of the political economy of Japan a decade earlier, if not the United States itself in the late 1920s. Surely the United States could not continue to consume beyond its means forever and run outsized balance-of-payments deficits. Yet no alarms were sounded by the celebrants of the American way who used U.S. power directly and through the global institutions to force others to adopt our form of deregulated capitalism. Only with the East Asian financial crisis did there begin to be a wider awareness that financial liberalization was creating financial crises and that these destabilizing events were becoming more common and destructive.

The uneven pattern of capitalist growth at the turn of the millennium is experienced as uncontrolled capital movements that destabilize economies and pose the difficulty of developing adjustment mechanisms. Economists understand this problem within the framework of the Mundell-Fleming model, which shows that governments, their economic policy makers, central bankers, and treasury officials cannot simultaneously maintain monetary policy independence, a stable exchange rate, and unrestricted capital movements. Two of these three are possible, not all simultaneously. Free capital flows and stable exchange rates can be achieved by allowing interest rates to move in line with external pressures. It is possible by controlling capital movements to have exchange rate stability and to control domestic interest rates, and of course if exchange rates are allowed to adjust to market forces then capital mobility and monetary autonomy are possible.

From a more forthright political perspective the question is even simpler: How can capital be brought under social control in the interest of employment security and working-class solidarity? Fiscal policy (taxation and government spending) is captive to international monetary pressures because capital's "freedom" in the form of flexible exchange rates and capital flows can make such policies ineffective. An open economy subservient to market forces reduces state economic policy autonomy and forces decision makers to adjust rather than to lead. They allow themselves to be constrained by markets rather than collectively regulating them. If they attempt activism without national controls and in the absence of an international governance structure that would place social purpose ahead of profit maximization, market pressures are likely to be destabilizing and regressively redistributional. Of course this is a matter of degree. Public pressure on governments can be important and effective. The greater the class-consciousness of working people, the harder it will be for amoral capital to prevail. The point though is that without the controls and social regulation, which need to be central to any "new financial architecture," governance is given, in

Keynes's words, to "a parliament of banks." We will continue to be faced with the need for painful adjustments and costly bailouts of financial speculators.

At the start of a new century the issue was not the threat of inflation but of deflation. While there had been little sign of inflation since the early 1980s when Reagan–Volcker policies raised interest rates (and unemployment) while cutting taxes for the corporate rich to stimulate a skewed growth pattern, monetarists of different stripes continued to press for the elimination of inflation. The evidence does not in fact even show that inflation is harmful to growth. Modest inflation, World Bank researchers tell us, has no discernible effects on economic growth. Working people are better off with some inflation and full employment under which their real incomes after inflation go up. The pursuit of lower inflation now threatens global deflation and has consequences that need to be better understood. Deflation, a drop in the general price level, makes it more difficult for debtors, including countries and corporations, to pay back debt, which is fixed in nominal terms. When this debt is in a foreign currency, and depreciation of one's own currency occurs it is even more difficult to pay debts. As financial liberalization has produced speculative bubbles followed by deflation country after country has had this experience.

Globalization as it proceeded has reversed price movements and although it is too early to say that future historians will look back at efforts to impose austerity as creating a dangerous deflationary situation, there is mounting evidence that this is becoming the case. The logic of financial hegemony has been to reduce government expenditures and state intervention through privatization and contracting out, and to do away with capital controls. The only element missing is the restoration of the gold standard. The demand for greater transparency and free trade is for operationalizing the idealized market mechanism, which is to automatically achieve optimal external and internal equilibrium, as in the textbook utopias of neoclassical economists. Orthodox policies once again, as before the Great Depression and the advent of Keynes, assert that interventionism by governments concerned to create jobs and adequate living standards will do more harm than good. Living standards suffer as a result. If hundreds of millions of people around

the world suffer because of the noninclusionary model of development
and the exploitative practices of capital and governments that not only
fail to regulate abuses of labor rights but are themselves guilty of human
rights abuses, the viability of life on the planet is also endangered by
policies that ignore the ecological costs of nonsustainable development.
The challenge for the global movement for social justice in the twenty-
first century is to articulate an inclusive version of sustainable development and articulate the goals, widen the consciousness raising, and
build the activism to achieve it.

Sustainable development includes social development, the eradica-
tion of poverty, and the full participation of the now marginalized
millions excluded from the possibilities inherent in an equitable model
of sustained growth. Respect for people and for the environment go
hand in hand, are interdependent, and need to be mutually reinforcing.
Fragile ecosystems are protected not only by denying the mindless
exploitation and rape of the wilderness, but also by sustaining community and preserving the vibrancy and biological diversity of our mutual
habitats. To protect natural resources and their sustainable use we must
foster alternative means of livelihood.

While attention is rightly given to protecting mountain ecosystems
and fragile semidesert areas, it is in the richest countries that the greatest
work needs to be done. The United States, with 5 percent of the world's
population, consumes a quarter of the world's energy and an even larger
proportion of the world's raw materials. It is a major contributor,
perhaps the greatest contributor, to the continued deterioration of the
global environment with its unsustainable pattern of consumption and
production. Other industrialized and industrializing nations will also
have to radically redesign what are unsustainable models of resource
usage and waste disposal. A redefinition of wealth and social cost, net
income, and future value calculation challenges conventional economic
thinking at the most basic level. These issues are part of a larger
conversation that can only grow more consequential.

Popular Resistance and Progressive Globalism

Despite the hegemonic position of transnational capital, its influence
over government and the media, most people reject its agenda and are

outraged by the impact of many of its policies. Opinion polls show that four out of five Americans would avoid shopping in a store that sells garments made with sweatshop labor and would pay a dollar more on a $20 item for a guarantee that the product came from a "worker-friendly" supplier. Companies know that their exploitative policies are unpopular and they are vulnerable when capitalism's business as usual can be dramatized in the mind of the public. The in-their-face militancy of grass-roots labor, environmental, and human rights groups has been able to do just this, dramatically and powerfully putting forward evidence that companies like Wal-Mart and Disney are greedy exploiters and urging people to stand up for worker rights.

That Disney pays six cents in Haiti for every garment it sells for $19.99 in this country and similar statistics popularized by groups like the National Labor Committee and the People of Faith Network using militant marches, demonstrations, leaflets, press conferences, and other consciousness-spreading tools, produce growing awareness of how existing capitalism operates. The Global Sweatshop Coalition of solidarity, justice groups, and trade unions impacts the public consciousness by bringing workers from El Salvador, Haiti, and Nicaragua to U.S. audiences. It built support for a "People's Right to Know Campaign" that calls for corporate disclosure—who makes products, where, and under what living and working conditions. Companies almost always have refused to release such information to consumers.

In the late 1990s and into the new century, colleges and universities were challenged to be sweatshop-free in their purchasing. As big corporations themselves many of them do not like this. Yet change has come about through ordinary people becoming involved. In 1999, Jim Keady, a former soccer star, assistant coach at St. John's University, and a theology student, was forced to resign for protesting the unethical relationship with Nike that his school had entered into, in which the company gave the school money and equipment and the coaches and players became moving billboards for products made in its sweatshops. Keady continued to speak out and challenge the morality of his school's deal with Nike (Nike has similar arrangements with over two hundred schools). In an effort to call attention to what life was like for many of Nike's half-million workers in subcontractor factories, Keady voluntarily lived for a month in Tangerang in worker housing on $1.20 a day, a factory worker's wage for sewing shoes for Nike. While in Indonesia he met with workers who told him of the harsh working and living conditions, fifteen-hour workdays, and starvation wages. As part of the same movement, Leo Johnson, a youth worker at the Edenwald-Gunhill Neighborhood Center in the Bronx, has inspired kids to refuse Nike sneakers (and to return their old pairs to the company) as a protest until Nike starts to pay all of its workers a living wage. A growing coalition of settlement houses and youth organizations is asking young people to face what Nike has done not only to its workers abroad but what Nike is doing to them—not only mercilessly advertising $150 shoes without which some refuse to go to school, for which others steal, but which are "sucking the brains out of their heads," in Johnson's words. At a gut level people understand that the fetishism of commodities is powerfully destructive of human potential. The anti-sweat shop coalition holding candle-lit marches from Niketown to the Disney store on New York's Fifth Avenue makes the connections well. Disney's upbeat, tirelessly promoted image of harmless consumer family values does not sit well with the reality of a greedy and exploitative company whose abuses range from its current attempt to bust the union of technical workers at its ABC-TV network to its sweatshops in Haiti.

Such companies scrambled for cover. They negotiated with the church and labor groups, the human rights and worker rights coalitions. But these meetings did not produce much real substance. They broke down when companies wanted a code of conduct that would allow them to employ fourteen-year-old children up to sixty hours a week at the local "legal" minimum wage (which are unlivable wages set by repressive governments to please these same corporations). The industry offer of independent monitors, who are beholden to the companies, instead of allowing inspection by movement groups themselves, and the limiting of inspection to 5 percent of a company's contractors in any given year, seemed like such a whitewash that the groups decided that no agreement was better than letting such companies use a "No Sweat" label in their garments to deceive consumers into thinking that they were treating workers fairly.

Indeed, two monitoring groups emerged from this conflict. The first is a Clinton White House–backed Fair Trade Association. The second is an activist-endorsed Workers Rights Consortium. Nike, to take one prominent example, is an enthusiastic member of the first and like many of the corporations criticized by activists worked first to prevent the independent monitoring and then to destroy the activists' organization. When the University of Oregon joined the Workers Rights Consortium, Phil Knight, Nike chairman and major stockholder, announced that he would not be giving a planned $30 million contribution to help his alma mater renovate its athletic stadium. He said the university was free to align itself with the Workers Rights Consortium (which has forty-five university members and monitors overseas factories where hats, T-shirts, and other apparel are made under license and carry a university logo), but that he preferred the Fair Trade Association, a group that student activists believed to be dominated by corporations and unlikely to be properly vigorous in its monitoring. Nike has been particularly critical of surprise visits, something the Fair Trade Association does not do. United Students Against Sweatshops, the umbrella group supporting the Workers Rights Consortium, which is backed by union groups, issued a report that coincided with Knight's announcement criticizing Nike for using sweatshops and especially faulted Nike's China facilities.[1]

The venue-shifting effort by industry in its attempts to bribe and otherwise pressure those seeking to improve working conditions and strengthen worker rights to abandon the more militant and uncompromising Workers Rights Consortium for the domesticated, industry-backed group is of a piece with corporations moving decision making out of the UN framework to the IMF and WTO where they had more control. The powerful seek to dominate the decision-making and regulatory forums, attempt to prevent independent scrutiny, and spend lavishly on public relations to avoid making substantial changes that would cut into their profits.

In 1998 Nike chief executive Phil Knight conceded that "the Nike product has become synonymous with slave wages, forced overtime, and arbitrary abuse." It was worth tens of millions of dollars to Nike to clean up its image and to keep sweatshop activists out of its factories, only admitting those monitors less likely to find abuses. A company's good name can be its most valuable asset. Indeed so important is it that when Andersen Consulting, for example, had to change its name after splitting from its parent company, Arthur Andersen, it spent $100 million on its rebranding exercise, employing seventy lawyers from twenty-four firms to check trademarks and Internet addresses. (They settled on Accenture.) Think how much more Nike and other consumer product companies are willing to pay for a better image.

The Streets of Seattle

The demonstrations at the World Trade Organization annual meeting from November 30 to December 3, 1999, were described as a major signaling event, a wake-up call for the 3,000 official delegates, 2,000 journalists, other registered observers, and hoards of media and the world, which watched as tens of thousands of protesters from all over the world denounced the organization. Estimates of the number of protesters ranged to 60,000 or more. What almost all of the participants wanted was a nonviolent protest of the corporate agenda the World Trade Organization was pursuing. What they got was tear gas, pepper spray, and the first use in American history of dangerous and painful rubber bullets against peaceful demonstrators. The movement in opposition to efforts of the global state governance institutions such as the World Trade Organization takeover of the management of the international economy may well be larger than any popular protest since the 1960s antiwar and civil rights movements.

President Clinton played a two-faced game, aware that his vice president's chances of succeeding him rested in the hands of the Democratic party's core constituencies and that these constituencies were in the streets of Seattle. The city's mayor, mindful that so much of the city supported the demonstrators and their concerns, despite the fact that they were told daily how important "free trade" was to their prosperity, did likewise. Clinton, who had up until Seattle spoken as if there were only two choices: free trade on capital's preferred terms or no trade (the alleged choice of the demonstrators), rhetorically moved to his familiar ploy of "feel your pain" politics, supporting environmental and labor rights issues without giving any substance to his rhetorical support.

Instead these issues were treated as side issues to be piously supported in preamble language while corporate freedom to pollute and exploit are given free rein. The battle in Seattle ended in decisive defeat for Clinton and a major gain in consciousness raising for the widely diverse movements represented in the protests. It became clear as Ellen Bernard, executive director of the Harvard Trade Union Program wrote in the *Washington Post*: "It's really not a question of free trade versus protectionism, but of who and what is free, and who and what is protected."[2]

In anticipation of the Seattle meeting some eight hundred grassroots organizations from over seventy-five countries had called for resistance to the growing power of corporate greed and to the WTO for contributing to the concentration of wealth, increasing poverty, and fostering an unsustainable pattern of production and consumption. They charge that the WTO's rules and procedures are undemocratic and marginalize the majority of the world's people who must live with the instability and social degradation that comes as a result of the acceleration of the process of globalization without social control. In the wake of Seattle this movement is stronger and more committed. It is likely to become even larger and more effective. While the majority of those in the streets were North Americans, the workers of the world were participating. The WTO has united farmers, workers, and citizens from around the planet. The success of the Seattle protests raised a number of questions: How would the emergent global social movement proceed? What demands would it make? What sort of politics would it embrace? How would it see change coming about? How would the activists relate to global state institutions?

Winning Universal Economic and Social Rights

Faced with massive politically organized popular demands, as they were with NAFTA in 1993, the Clinton administration assuaged protests with a promise of "side agreements" to the treaty, which the president said would meet the objections. Some years later these side agreements on labor and the environment are widely agreed to be ineffective. When the WTO was established in 1995, environmentalists demanded and got an environmental working group in the WTO. This working group turned out to be trade-oriented, studying environmental laws "not to safeguard them but rather to figure out how to get rid of them," as Lori Wallach, director of Public Citizen's Global Trade Watch, tells us. There is a long history of rhetorical concessions and empty reforms as a way of better perpetuating injustice. In effect this working group represents another instance of venue shifting. Rather than allowing environmentalists, NGOs, and environmental ministers from the world's governments to work out the protection of the environment, and have WTO agreements on trade subservient to these treaties, the WTO sets up an in-house body to cool out protesters. Thus "side agreements" and "study groups" delay while the agenda of transnational capital gets fast-tracked.

International Labor Organization (ILO) conventions ban child labor and give approval to the rights of association. But the ILO depends on voluntary compliance. It has no enforcement powers. The World Trade Organization of course does. It could compel and enforce labor standards as it does intellectual property rights and such. But it chooses not to because . . . . well, because these issues fall within the jurisdiction of the ILO! It is perhaps useful to remember that the ILO was formed in 1919 to prevent the spread of Bolshevik influence among the workers of the world, especially those of Europe where the appeal was quite substantial. The ILO is the only international governance organization that has a tripartite structure. The corporations closely collaborate with organized labor and governments to pursue noble goals that cannot be enforced by the organization. The ILO relies on moral suasion and embarrassment as its weapon. The WTO of course does not have a tripartite structure. Labor is not a partner. The WTO can tell states what they must do, typically at the behest of the most powerful transnational corporations. The relationship between the ILO and the WTO with regard to labor rights involves both venue shifting and venue trumping. Unable to avoid any discussion of labor rights, the ILO is set up with a talk shop having no real power. Discussion of labor rights issues is then confined as much as possible to the ILO ("That is the ILO's mandate, let them deal with it"). This shifts the discussion to the venue that cannot do much to change conditions (venue shifting). The decisions that affect working conditions are called trade issues and the WTO as a venue has the real power. This represents venue trumping. The WTO can enforce its decisions and they are made supposedly on criteria of economic efficiency that thus trump labor rights as the priority in global governance.

While the WTO Secretariat *Report on Trade and Investment* argues that "a lack of rule policy and coherence" pose a "danger to security and stability, which are basic goals of trade and investment agreements," and that such coherence extends to a very broad variety of investment-related policies from trademark enforcement to protecting the rights of foreign producers in a host of specific ways, it also says that the protection of workers' property in their ability to determine the conditions under which they labor is not trade related, not the business of the WTO, which could do something about it, but of the ILO. Of course without continued "street heat" as part of a political movement too substantial to ignore, a working group on labor standards is unlikely to bring about much in the way of real labor rights for the working people of the world. Such victories will be won against the WTO and the transnational corporations for which it exists through struggle rather than through real dialogue with them.

Such outside pressure to some extent changes the way things work inside international organizations. The ILO in 1999 got a new director, its first from the Third World. He was committed to activism and perhaps the ILO can become a relatively more powerful vehicle for the pursuance of working-class interests. But the real action is elsewhere in the same way that the United Nations General Assembly is allowed to debate while economic issues are decided in other forums such as the World Bank and the International Monetary Fund where it is not one nation, one vote, but one dollar, one vote and the United States alone has sufficient "votes" for veto power. The advanced countries are already in compliance with the ILO labor standards even if in practice some, most prominently the British and the Americans, have been most actively undercutting labor rights. Labor standards give them a stick with which to beat the East Asian and other newly industrializing economies. The developing countries that strongly object to labor standards do so not of course because they are concerned with labor rights. They share with the advanced economies' governments the goal of maximizing capital accumulation, but for their capitalists. They are also not advocates for livable wages and better working conditions or any rights for their workers.

To help us understand what is going on, consider the distinction between labor standards and labor rights. Labor standards are externally determined yardsticks that are, or can be, used to exclude the products of particular countries from other markets. Labor rights are about the responsibilities of employers and governments to respect workers and their organizations. Above all they are about the power of self-organization of the working class and the capacity to redefine the rules governing capital and labor relations because they have the power to do so. Labor standards are granted. Labor rights are won. Labor's friends can be important contributors to the achievement of both. But the emphasis is different. Labor standards, where they are formally accepted, leave terrible practices untouched in the largest sector of the economies that do not produce for export but cater to the domestic economy. There are no international sanctions proposed to help these workers. They can only be helped by the winning of labor rights. Labor standards in any case are enforced typically by governments or self-policing trade groups and not by independent union monitoring. External agencies focus on symbolic standards issues. What is finally more important is the self-organization of the workers and empowering their independent organizations. Advocacy of labor standards generates space in the public arena. Strategically it needs to be seen as a step toward winning labor rights. Labor standards have been common ground on which traditional union concerns and a broader human rights agenda meet. If trade unions have increasingly learned to deal with their members as whole people, with race, ethnicity, and gender identities, social movements have been slower to see the centrality of work life. By the end of the twentieth century some impressive learning was evident.

Trade unions are not represented at the WTO, where government representatives bristle at any mention of enforcing labor rights. They see this as "protectionism" by the advanced economies, an effort to keep them poor. Workers in these countries do not feel this way, however. Congressman Sherrod Brown, a member of the House International Relations Committee, responding to a *Business Week* editorial, "What Developing Countries Want," informed the readers of that publication that "During the World Trade Organization talks in Seattle, I met with a trade minister from an 'Asian tiger' nation. He told me that his government would never accept international labor standards. When I asked him if he knew the opinion of his nation's trade unions (which are repressed in his and most other developing nations), he replied testily: 'They would probably want labor standards.' " [3]

The basic problem for workers in both the developed and the developing countries is not foreign competition but the power of capital. Jobs need protecting because capital creates and maintains coercive pressure on labor, uses state power and the so-called freedom of the marketplace to escape social control to the maximum degree possible. Capital keeps workers competing as best it can and attempts to erode class-consciousness and working-class power. If the concern is the social conditions of workers then the focus of public policy would not be on subsidies that favor capital, write-offs for machinery, and other favorable tax treatment when plants are closed for industry, but that leave workers stranded. It is the lack of adequate spending on job creation, health, and education for working-class families, and the taxation and regulation of capital that should be the focus of governmental attention. The struggle for labor standards can be an important way to place some limits on capital in industrializing countries and to raise consciousness concerning the extent of exploitation and oppression, but the struggle must also be for working-class power. This requires labor movements that are organized by workers themselves with as much support as possible from other progressive movements, not simply the adoption of standards without enforcement mechanisms. The pullout of progressive forces that had been addressing problems of Third World sweatshops by negotiating with producers over codes of conduct came about precisely because industry dominated. Limited inspection was seen not as a tool in forwarding labor rights but as a public relations vehicle for the large transnationals involved who had been embarrassed by unflattering publicity and hoped to escape more meaningful scrutiny. The lesson to be learned is that labor rights are won by building a sustained and deeper awareness of how capitalism works as well as a counter-hegemonic movement capable of transforming class society.

If there is no overwhelming interest on the part of the international organizations with real power to struggle for protecting the environment and the emancipation of labor, some agencies of corporate globalism are very much involved in pursuing the emancipation of capital from popular control. The Multilateral Agreement on Investment, which had been negotiated in secret for years, and which *Business Week* called "The Explosive Trade Deal You've Never Heard Of," was unknown until Public Citizen Global Trade Watch put a draft of the agreement on the World Wide Web. Renato Ruggiero, the then Director General of the WTO, describes the Multilateral Agreement on Investment proposal as the "constitution for a single global economy." It took the principles enshrined in the North American Free Trade Agreement and the World Trade Organization to a higher level, requiring governments to make no new laws that interfere with the right of capital to free investment where and when it likes and to roll back existing restrictions on capital. The rules also required a five-year period before any country could withdraw from the agreement and another fifteen years until any changes could be made to corporate protections and privileges. Nations would lose control over their economies and could be sued for interfering with transnationals and would have to pay penalties if their policies cost companies forgone profit. Widespread popular opposition and the resistance of several governments forced the withdrawal of the Multilateral Agreement on Investment proposal. But its logic still pervades the United States–led negotiations to develop a new international economic regime.

It is surely clear that capital is attempting to create an international state with powers unaccountable to elected governments and obeying only the rule of the marketplace as defined by transnational capital. Its bureaucratic allies are being empowered by states that would not attempt to carry out such policies on their own. They have to face reelection. By saying "It is out of our hands," and "Globalization is beyond anything we can do anything about" they willingly surrender sovereignty to capital. Only organized opposition with class-conscious awareness of what is at stake can reverse these developments. The problem is not that we are part of a globalized society, but that we are part of a global capitalist society. This is increasingly clear to popular movements that are mobilizing to challenge the world's most powerful corporations.

Awareness of the real issues is spreading and movements in different parts of the world are in closer contact. This has contributed to a change in ruling-class tactics. The problem in the advanced countries is not Thatcher-Reagan attacks on the working class and its organizations. The appeal of harsh anti-working-class governments has diminished as the cost of their policies become widely experienced and understood. The Clinton approach was to feel workers' pain, to preach democracy, and to convince us that there is no choice but neoliberalism with a smiley face. The Bush administration tells us market outcomes are just and government should just leave people alone—by which it means let corporate power structure decisions, not democracy. This shift may represent the construction of new international regime rules, the positive moment that may be the consolidation of the era of globalization into a Davos-style globality or very different possibilities, depending on the nature and extent of popular struggles.

Agendas

What fuels fundamental social change is a radical vision shared widely that motivates mass political activity. It is not enough to be oppressed or to be upset by the exploitation one sees around one. In the absence of hope for meaningful change, a sense that a better alternative exists and is possible, pessimism and cynicism prevail. A radical vision then consists first of anger at the way things are, allowing oneself to feel that conditions are intolerable. But if this is to lead beyond rebellion, the anger must be accompanied by a belief that a better alternative is not only desirable but possible, not necessarily tomorrow, but that the momentum can be turned around. Resistance can have a strong element of moral witness (speaking truth to power), of rebellion (I'm mad and I won't take it any more), of reformist goals (our mutual ideals are violated, let us live up to our agreed-upon principles as in the adoption of the Universal Declaration of Human Rights), and of revolutionary transformation (the institutions of structured inequality and destructiveness are necessary to preserve their power; the system must be overthrown and a fundamentally different one put in its place). At the deepest level the task is to retain the mutual respect for life and wholeness that has been at the heart of the world's great religions and participatory democratic political movements.

Whenever capital is seen to overreach and in its greed endanger even the sustainability and the reproduction of the system two impulses come to the fore in terms of redress. From reformers both inside and outside the system comes a desire to solve the immediately pressing problem by making changes that allow the system to work better: fuller disclosure and more open access with the implicit promise that sunshine is the best disinfectant. Whether financial market allocation or democratic policy making, better information allows for better decisions. The second impulse is to transform existing social relations of hierarchical power, to take away power that has been abused, to penalize usurpers, seize back what has been illegitimately expropriated, to break the authority relation of coercive domination that allows and encourages the intolerable outcomes.

In the first approach, structures of power are left in place so that as soon as the crisis is perceived to have passed or diminished in intensity the tentacles reach out once more. Business as usual resumes, perhaps with greater care to observe, for public consumption, the niceties of verbal allegiance to the key words of the movement. It is in just such a fashion that the very word democracy, an insulting word to describe the rule of the unwashed mob, became a revered ideal of state elites. Over time there is erosion of social control and the philosophy of reform gives way to the necessities of realism, the drive to accumulate. Beyond that, as memory of the crisis fades, the moment of popular empowerment and systemic challenge to the reign, capitalist logic resumes to the extent that it can once again be said, "there is no alternative." Reforms do not last unless a mobilized powerful movement keeps the pressure on and the momentum going.

Venue Shifting and the United Nations

To understand how the political struggle over whose globalization agenda will dominate is likely to proceed consider what is at this writing a new development in the debate, the initiative by the United Nations Secretary General Kofi Annan first put forward in Davos in 1999, to create a voluntary Global Compact, an alliance between the UN and the transnational corporations who would promise to follow good global citizen guidelines. It is possible that if deadlock continues at the WTO, and if the IMF and WB no longer are able to effectively shape domestic economies of dependent countries, those who had sought to use those venues may turn to the United Nations seeking legitimacy for their designs and cover for their actions. Were this to happen a host of issues relating to global financial stability and economic development could find their way onto the agenda of a differently empowered UN. But it is also possible that the executive of the UN, the office of the secretary general, who, as the ignominious dumping of Boutros Boutros Gali demonstrates, serves at the pleasure of the UN's most powerful, if still deadbeat member, could house new initiates congenial to transnational capital's interests. Indeed, such an effort appears to have been launched with Annan's announcement of a Global Compact. How the social movements react to such a proposal will depend on how much trust they have in the kind of procedure it represents.

The Global Compact is a voluntary instrument to promote corporate responsibility. Far from being regulatory, the compact would identify and disseminate good practices based on universal principles. Transnationals are invited to commit themselves to these and report at least once a year on concrete steps they are taking to act out the nine principles. The nine principles are derived from the Universal Declaration of Human Rights, the 1992 Rio Declaration of the United Nations Conference on Environment and Development, the fundamental principles and rights at work adopted at the World Economic and Social Summit in Copenhagen in 1997 and reaffirmed by the ILO in 1999. Good principles all. They are also invited to pay to fund the project.

This endeavor may be, as the secretary general asserts, an effort at stimulating compliance with labor and environmental standards by the transnational corporations, or it may be a mechanism to offer cover to these firms now on the defensive from charges made against their activities in these areas. Annan and John Ruggie, chief adviser on the effort, understand the reason some companies might sign on: "The most encompassing is the protection and promotion of the company brand which accounts for an ever increasing, and in some cases overwhelming, share of companies' market valuation. Some companies have done bad in the past, they've paid a price in public embarrassment and perhaps even diminished sales, and they want a new image." He understands that there are those for whom it is all about image. They are looking for a free ride off the UN's good name and may have little intention of changing their stripes. But, he said, "We are alert. Our NGO and labor partners are watching." Besides, he admits the UN doesn't have the resources to monitor compliance and certainly no power to enforce the standards. Ruggie knows movement people will be suspicious. But, he asks, what real choice is there? The transnational corporations inevitably have the power, in his view not least because the world needs open markets to sustain the prosperity of the advanced economies and to spread it to the less developed nations. They therefore provide the only hope of pulling billions of people out of abject poverty. In Ruggie's view the "rejectionists" in the north are driven by a cultural alienation from the institutions and practices that generate wealth. They are, in the view of Professor Ruggie, on a collision course with the world's poor.

To many NGOs, matters looked quite different. As a Corporate Watch Statement of October 2000 declares: "The UNDP—the United Nations Development Programme — is selling global corporations its international network of offices, high level governmental contacts and its reputation at a bargain price. At $50,000 apiece, companies like Citibank and the British mining conglomerate Rio Tinto have signed up as sponsors of a 'poverty alleviation' program that promises to brighten their images far more than it would serve the needs of the world's least fortunate people." The companies were enjoying the opportunity to "greenwash" or "bluewash" their images on the cheap, in the view of Corporate Watch and other NGOs. The UN's positive image would suffer, sullied by covering for corporate criminals. It was suggested that companies that violate human rights and the other principles of the compact should not be allowed to join. The corporate partnership represents the UN taking the low road with transnational corporations.

Whether the UN leadership is acting opportunistically and in effect offering cover to the transnational corporations willing to pony up some money and make some innocuous promises that will be neither monitored nor enforced, or whether this is in some sense beginning with a non-threatening device in order to eventually gain some real leverage, remains to be seen. In this context we may quote Bernie Sanders, Vermont's independent socialist congressman, quoting "a wise friend" who shares an enduring truth that important change nearly always begins in hypocrisy. Writing at a moment of activism in the streets and platitude in the suites, Sanders notes: "The international flurry of high-level solicitude invites cynicism, since it's clearly intended to reassure the general public (never mind the activists) that conscientious firms and institutions are on the case, diligently cleaning up the global system, so there's no need for any intrusive laws from governments. But each self-righteous claim offers a new target for agitation." So should social movements support such initiatives as the Global Compact? It is clear that for the UN such initiatives may represent progress. They are a way of getting the attention and involvement of the transnational corporations that have previously ignored the UN and gone about their business any way they liked. When the Third World countries tried to adopt codes of conduct for multinational corporations in the 1970s, the United States and the other powerful countries of the core put a stop to such efforts. The Global Compact, modest as it appears, gets the UN back into the game, makes it a little more relevant to how real power is exercised by corporations. From the perspective of the executive of a global governance institution with little real power over the global political economy, this is a step forward. But what about the social movements? Should they see this as progress or an attempt to co-opt more meaningful change? Or both?

A Constitutionalism for Progressive Globalism?

When powerful movements from below are in motion the powerful are persuaded to say the appropriate words as a sign of at least a verbal commitment to higher values and decent behavior. If the movement pounds them hard enough, the rules that could not be changed are modified in direct proportion to the pressure from below and the degree of popular consciousness and commitment. If people settle for less they get still less. It is not really what the powerful can afford to give in some precisely measurable sense but rather what they must give, what they can be forced to concede. In the "fix it or nix it" debate the movement has carried on, the real core question is can any movement strong enough to nix it create a very different alternative? To really fix these institutions would be even more difficult since it would involve technical discussion that by its nature demobilizes the mass base. Attempting to fix these institutions may save them, while a frontal and sustained attack on their rationale and operation, with ongoing education and consciousness raising, may instigate more fundamental change.

It is in this spirit that Walden Bello, speaking in Prague, asked if movement leaders will they allow themselves to be sucked into a process of "reasonable dialogue" and "frank consultation" when the other side sees the dialogue and consultation "mainly as a first step to the disarmament of the other side." He has suggested directing the movement's fire against the transnational corporations, which are "the fortresses and earthworks" constituting the core of the global economic system. In a similar vein Colin Lloyd writes, "When we say: 'Destroy the IMF' and reject the strategy of dialogue and piecemeal reform it is because the project of reforming global capital is a Utopia. That will not stop us from fighting for partial and immediate demands like the dropping of all debt without condition, and massive reparations from the IMF/World Bank to the Third World countries they have plundered." He calls for wealth in the hands of those who actually create it. Whether these more revolutionary positions gain strength in what is a broad and amorphous coalition remains to be seen. It will be an interesting political debate.

It is not that the Global Compact does not ask for commitment to good values. It is rather that the UN has no power to enforce these standards on corporations. The compact leaves it up to corporations. It relies on popular pressure for any real progress. The task therefore remains to keep the pressure on. Nonetheless, the noble ideals enshrined in the various UN documents do constitute an alternative constitution to the one being imposed by neoliberalism. As long as we remember that what counts is the militancy of the movement struggling to achieve these noble principles it is helpful to expand our consideration by taking a closer look at them. The most impressive of these, more than a century after its adoption, is the Universal Declaration of Human Rights, which marked its fiftieth anniversary in 1948. Because of this document, many people have had the opportunity to learn about their own fundamental civil, political, and economic rights, which suggests that there is opportunity to build a progressive alternative constitutionalism for the emergent global economy based on this wonderful document. (Indeed, ten million people signed Amnesty International's pledge to do what they can to implement the declaration.) What tenets can be suggested for a people's constitutionalism on the basis of this document compared to the constitutionalism of the proposed Multilateral Agreement on Investment and the legal framework urged by transnational capital? In a sense the program is not as important as the movement. Ideas alone do not change the world. Only an organized and politically conscious movement can do that. But a vision of alternative futures is needed. People must be able to envision the broad shape of a better future and believe it is attainable. What if we modeled a constitutionalism for a globalized economy on the Universal Declaration of Human Rights? What if working people refused to give electoral support to parties that represent the interests of the transnational corporations and international finance?

Existing law reifies corporations, granting them personhood and citizenship while denying to citizens the right to personhood, to a livable wage, employment security and other requisites presumably guaranteed fifty years ago at the founding of the United Nations. If the goal of production is to meet human needs, then performance requirements applied to economic entities should primarily protect not capital, but workers, consumers, communities and the rest of the living environment. This would require not so much a radical shift in the balance of power back to government, but a different class base of support of a governance framework. Progressive politics would require a reconceptualization of the function of government in class terms, a move from privatization to socialization (economic activity based on social purpose and not nationalization under which governments run enterprises purely as businesses), globally oriented reregulation in place of deregulation under a broader understanding of the purpose of societal control, and a move to replace structural adjustment with structural transformation.

The problem is that capital's hegemony extends to control of the political process. Voters are often not given the choices that they require. At the level of ideas and building counter-hegemony, a movement strong enough to be taken seriously could pose specific alternatives. One might be the revival of the UN draft Code of Conduct on Multinational Corporations with its enumeration of rights and obligations for companies and governments. Voters in each country could read a draft of the Multilateral Agreement on Investment and of the UN Code of Conduct and choose one approach over the other. More democratic countries might want to decide that corporations could not spend money in self-serving efforts to sway the vote, although they could send representatives to speak at local forums in which people could ask questions and make comments in town-meeting fashion.

We are a long way from this sort of possibility. It is inconceivable that the capitalist version of democracy would want to offer such a choice. But we need to ask why should basic democracy seem beyond the demands citizens can justifiably make? Whereas under the proposed MAI corporations could sue for compensation if they lost any profit after governments restricted their freedom, under democratic governance guidelines workers and communities could sue corporations who left workers and taxpayers in the lurch after taking tax incentives. People whose ancestors were brought to this country in involuntary servitude could sue for back wages, Native Americans whose land was taken, Latin American countries whose gold was removed to Europe (as perhaps a long-term loan) might demand debt repayment at appropriate interest. The MAI idea offers endless reversal parallels to address long-standing injustices. The stolen cultures, the young people forcibly indoctrinated into consumers willing to steal for sneakers and the burdened parents who feel forced to buy sneakers rather than pay the phone bill could seek redress. In the American tradition we can suggest legal action based on new grounds that would have legal standing in the new dispensation of exploitation mental anguish. That all of this seems so unlikely is a measure of the hegemony of capitalist ideology. It would require a revolution.

It is difficult to keep in mind, because this is not the way we are educated and encouraged to think, that there have been powerful revolutions in history. Once kings ruled by what was thought to be divine right. Human beings owned other human beings and, it was said, the practice was a natural one, sanctioned by the Bible itself. Once only property-owning white males could vote. Not so very long ago black Americans had to sit in the back of the bus and women were told they couldn't be doctors, lawyers, mathematicians, or scientists. There have been many revolutions. Each one inconceivable, impossible before they happened—and then, in retrospect, understood to have been inevitable. The revolution that brings about economic democracy will be similar. It may be called socialism. It may simply be the fulfillment of the promises of the world's great religions. It is not really so hard to think about swapping the rule of gold (those who have the gold make the rules) for the golden rule—to do onto others as you would have them do onto you.

The basic ideas are simple enough. Citizens could demand structural changes in economic relations to comply, as I've suggested, with the principles of the Universal Declaration of Human Rights. Written in a postwar period of great energy devoted to seeing that humans would be wiser in the future and avoid the causes of war, it declared that everyone has the right to work, to free choice of employment, to just and favorable conditions of work, and to protection against unemployment. That is all in Article 23. "Everyone who works has the right to just and favorable remuneration ensuring for himself [which we now understand can be read as himself or herself] and his [or her] family an existence worthy of human dignity, and supplemented, if necessary, by other means of social protection." Moving on from Article 24 to 25: "Everyone has the right to a standard of living adequate for the health and well-being of himself and his family [sic again] including food, clothing, housing and medical care . . . " Well, you get the idea. It is all there and can be accessed on the Amnesty International web page or that of the United Nations itself.

In an age in which capital's audacity seems boundless in its efforts to impose a new feudalism, in which the masters of the universe can use an internationalized state and its local subsidiaries to remake the world in their image, it does not seem amiss to celebrate the fiftieth anniversary of the Universal Declaration of Human Rights, to remind ourselves what the global financial institutions, the transnational corporations, and the governments that do their bidding are attempting to steal. People's rights come before capital's. It is also a good time to remember that it is not charters and declarations, however inspiring their words may be, that alone can make the difference. It is the organization of class-conscious political movements that know what they want and are willing to struggle to achieve their goals. Governments adopting resolutions, even when done with pure intentions, can hardly make the difference. Indeed, the United Nations High Commissioner for Human Rights, Mary Robinson, has said she does not celebrate the declaration because as she looks around the world she sees so many terrible things happening that she is unwilling to celebrate the declaration's fiftieth birthday, but only to mark it. In that spirit of interrogating the world with more educated eyes comes judgments of not only amoral behavior but also what can be understood as immoral behavior. The moral critique of our economic system by the global movement for social justice, which through this book has been contrasted with the "official" story, suggests that if we hold the global state economic governance institutions and the leaders of the world's governments to the standards of the Universal Declaration of Human Rights, which they and the societies of the world claim to endorse, the hypocrisy surrounding the celebration of global capitalism's triumph rings hollow indeed.

The world's richest 20 percent now receive 86 percent of the world's gross domestic product, the poorest 20 percent have only 1 percent, and the middle 60 percent just 13 percent. The world's richest two hundred people saw their incomes double between 1994 and 1998 to over a trillion dollars. The world's richest three people have assets greater than the combined output of the forty-eight poorest countries. Isn't a little mild reform called for? Could a little progressive taxation help? Could a tad of redistribution easily end mass suffering in the world? Consider: the 1999 United Nations *World Development Report* says that for $40 billion, basic health and nutrition, basic education, water sanitation, reproductive health, and family planning could be extended to the entire world's population. Could such a paltry sum possibly be raised? The report suggests that a yearly contribution of 1 percent of the wealth of the two hundred richest people (about $7 billion) could provide universal access to primary education. 5 percent would pay for all the basic social services. A Tobin Tax on all international financial transactions would raise $45 billion a month, and then there are those military budgets. Finding the money hardly seems a problem. Getting those who have it now to give it up, ah, there's a problem.

Partly this is an information problem. Take the Tobin tax idea that would place a tax on financial transactions. It would be small so as not to discourage long-term investment, but would represent a disincentive for very short-term speculative capital movements that move in and out of a currency or a country to take advantage of small temporary differentials. This "sand in the wheels" of such speculative movements might reduce to some extent their destabilizing impacts and in the process would raise huge amounts of money that could be earmarked for developmental purposes. Few Americans have heard of the Tobin tax. Yet in France there are 30,000 people who are members of Attac, the Association for the Taxation of Financial Transactions for the Aid of Citizens, and the group is considered a serious movement with supporters in parliament.

The problem is that seemingly reasonable changes supported by most people (whenever ordinary people are in fact asked) conflict with the logic of the way capitalism allocates resources. Once exceptions are made, where would they stop? There is no reason to think that compulsory licensing of AIDS drugs might not lead to the demand that all the people of the world who need medicines that can ease suffering and allow less pain should not have access to them. When we accept that since the most indebted countries cannot pay foreign debts these should simply be written off, what kind of precedent is set for future loans and the whole system of debt peonage? It is the suffering of those who fail to meet the system's demands that after all keep others in line. Instead of a beautiful elephant the existing system comes to be seen in more monstrous form. The questions the movement for social justice is asking have disquieting potential for the more prosperous. Even the "have-somethings" fear changes demanded by and on behalf of the have-nots. Such divisive fears are real enough and are fanned by the principalities and powers of the world.

In Chapter Three the historical parallel between the political economy of the merger movement at the turn of the twentieth century and the significance of the comparable era of global consolidation at the turn of the twenty-first century were discussed. What hope is there that at the next turn of the century mark some of the goals of the global social justice movement will have been achieved? In one such centennial Richard Rorty, looking backward from the perspective of the year 2096, writes:

> Just as twentieth-century Americans had trouble imagining how their pre-Civil War ancestors could have stomached slavery, so we at the end of the twenty-first century have trouble imagining how our great-grandparents could have legally permitted a CEO to get twenty times more than her lowest paid employees. We cannot understand how Americans a hundred years ago could have tolerated the horrific contrast between a childhood spent in the suburbs and one spent in the ghettos. Such inequalities seem to us evident moral abominations, but the vast majority of our ancestors took them to be regrettable necessities.[4]

What was most profoundly wrong in the mid-1990s, Rorty wrote in an essay calling for a return to class politics, was "the fact that people are now once again willing to cross picket lines, and are unwilling to ask themselves who makes their clothes or who picks their vegetables . . ."[5] In the years since that essay was written, a new generation of students and a reenergized broader movement have been increasingly visible in confronting just such moral lapses. The erosion of social solidarities has produced reaction in the form of militant confrontations and spirited protests as well as a general awareness of what has been lost in the decades of attacks upon and erosion of the social democratic class compromise.

By the 1980s and 1990s the New Deal structural reforms that protected capital from itself and to an important extent the rest of us from the worst excesses of capitalism without social regulation and that opened space for a somewhat more inclusive distribution of society's product had lost much of their original substance, had been defunded, deregulated, and neoliberalized. Its reformist regulatory agencies came to be headed by individuals whose goals were to sabotage their stated original purposes. At a structural level the forces of production, never divorced in any event from social relations, developed in new directions, empowering new fractions of capital and encouraging shifts within the historic bloc of capitalist domination both domestically and internationally. In many ways and in many places they have created intolerable conditions for people and the planet. In response one of the broadest based movements for social, economic, and political change the world has seen is being created to contest capital's version of globalization. One would not want to overstate the case. On the other hand it is also difficult to read turning points.

Seattle may prove to be just such an event. The WTO and police action in their attempts to squash dissent created lifetime activists who, as one participant, Kelly Quirke, executive director of the Rainforest Action Network, said in a web posting, got a real-life glimpse of what corporate-controlled reality looks like. Police in the streets, no civil rights, martial law, jail brutality: "we saw that what we jump-started the week with: an action warning about the loss of democracy is not just activist rhetoric, not just some advertisement, but real. We saw, all week long, as did the rest of the world, what they will do to get their way. But this is only the glimpse of A future, not THE future. All week long we also saw us. In the streets, counting on each other, trusting each other, loving each other. Determined, utterly determined, to create a world where reverence is what we practice, with work that fulfills us; building communities based on interdependence and cooperation and nurturing relationships that breathe passion into our lives." The announcement of a commitment to make it so came through loud and clear. In making an overall assessment we should perhaps take to heart the quintessentially American framing of John Sellers of the Berkeley-based Ruckus Society, one of the groups that coordinated the Seattle protest: "We just hit the big hoop at the halftime buzzer. But dude, this game is not over."

We cannot now know what difference the battle in Seattle will make. We can say that many of the demands raised there were and are "non-reformist reforms" in Andre Gorz's meaning of ones that do not base their validity and right to exist on capitalist needs, criteria, or rationales. Some are critiques (which so enraged the ideologues of the system cited at the start of this essay) of the productivism of the drive to accumulate for the sake of expansion of capital regardless of the cost to workers, the environment, or the community. They are also driven by a positive counter-vision of sustainability and social justice. A number of the protesting themes involve the rejection of capitalism's economic reasoning. The victories in the streets of Seattle, the resistance of other nations to the domination of the United States in the negotiations, and the gains in public awareness concerning the functions of the WTO in the global capitalist system, mark the beginning of a change in perception and have prompted outrage on the part of elite opinion molders.

We cannot very well change the world if we do not first understand it better. The task is not to understand simply the sake of understanding, but in order to be better prepared as we engage in the struggle for progressive social change. I would conclude then, as I began, by reasserting that in the current situation of increased globalization, the universalization of capital is a long-standing process, but one that takes on specific meanings in our time. Rank-and-file citizens of the world must have a position not simply on trade issues and collective bargaining, but a political position on capital controls and other legislation that empowers progressive politics by limiting the power of finance capital. We are being forced by history to learn to think in systemic terms. Were we to do so with any consistency, we would be drawn to a return as well to our more radical social traditions.

Notes

Chapter 1

1. Thomas L. Friedman, "Senseless in Seattle," *New York Times*, December 1, 1999.

2. "The Real Losers," *The Economist*, December 11, 1999.

3. Martin Wolf, "WHO: In Defense of Global Capitalism," *Financial Times*, December 8, 1999.

4. Martin Wolf, "Kicking Down Growth's Ladder," *Financial Times*, April 14, 2000.

5. <http://oneworld.org/campaigns/wto/wtoindia.html> and <http://www.agp.org>

6. Interview with Vandana Shiva, April 14, 2000, by Sheri Herndon from <www.in-dymedia.org>

7. Andrew Kohut, "Globalization and the Wage Gap," *New York Times*, December 3, 1999, and Albert R. Hunt, "A Flawed Protest Actually Produces Some Good Results," *Wall Street Journal*, April 20, 2000.

8. "What's Behind the Global Backlash," Editorial, *Business Week*, April 24, 2000.

9. Ibid.

10. Ibid.

11. Peter Aspden, "The Epitome of His Own Catch Phrase," *Financial Times*, March 14–15, 1998.

12. George Soros, "The International Crisis: An Interview," *New York Review of Books*, January 14, 1999.

13. Ibid.

14. "The 21st Century Economy," *Business Week*, August 31, 1998.

15. Richard Waters, "10,001: A Stock Odyssey," *Financial Times*, March 17, 1999.

16. James M. Poterba and Andrew A. Samwick, *Brookings Papers on Economic Activity* (1995), p. 2.

17. "Two-Tier Marketing," *Business Week*, March 17, 1997.

18. "Executive Pay: It's Out of Control," *Business Week,* April 12, 1997.

19. "Economic Anxiety," *Business Week,* March 11, 1996.

20. Louis Uchitelle, "More Downsized Workers Are Returning as Rentals," *New York Times,* December 8, 1996.

21. "Could It Happen Again?" *The Economist,* February 20, 1999.

22. David S. Landes, *The Unbound Prometheus: Technological Change and Industrial Development in Western Europe from 1750 to the Present* (Cambridge: Cambridge University Press, 1969), p. 3.

23. Ibid., p. 57.

24. Karl Marx and Friedrich Engels, *The Communist Manifesto* (New York: Monthly Review Press, 1968), pp. 4–12.

CHAPTER 2

1. Giovanni Arrighi, *The Long Twentieth Century: Money, Power, and the Origins of Our Times* (London: Verso, 1994), p. 300.

2. Fernand Braudel, *The Structures of Everyday Life* (New York: Harper and Row, 1981), p. 24.

3. Immanuel Wallerstein, in *The Capitalist World-Economy* (Cambridge: Cambridge University Press, 1979), p. 19.

4. Arrighi, op. cit., p. 45.

5. Carlos Marichal, *A Century of Debt Crisis in Latin America: From Independence to the Great Depression, 1820–1930* (Princeton: Princeton University Press, 1989), p. 5.

6. Karl Marx, *Capital: A Critical Analysis of Capitalist Production, Volume I* (New York: International Publishers, 1967), pp. 754–5.

7. Ibid., p. 756.

8. Karl Polanyi, *The Great Transformation: The Political and Economic Origins of Our Time* (Boston: Beacon Press, 1957), p. 14.

9. Ibid., p. 14.

10. Harry Magdoff, "Imperialism without Colonies," in *Imperialism: From the Colonial Age to the Present* (New York: Monthly Review Press, 1978), p. 120.

11. Daniel Boorstin, "Editor's Preface," to Samuel P. Hays, *The Response to Industrialism, 1885–1914* (Chicago: University of Chicago Press, 1957), p. vii.

12. Richard B. DuBoff, *Accumulation and Power: An Economic History of the United States* (Armonk: M. E. Sharpe, 1989).

13. Samuel P. Hays, *The Response to Industrialism, 1885–1914* (Chicago: University of Chicago Press, 1957), p. 1.

14. Jean Strouse, *Morgan: American Financier* (New York: Random House, 1999), p. 8.

15. Ron Chernow, *The House of Morgan: An American Banking Dynasty and the Rise of Modern Finance* (New York: Atlantic Monthly Press, 1998), p. 82.

16. Ibid., p. 181.

17. Ibid., p. 182.

18. Ibid., p. 131.

19. Ibid., p. 282.

CHAPTER 3

1. Jeffrey Sachs, "The IMF and the Asian Flu," *The American Prospect*, March-April 1998.

2. Arthur MacEwan, "Comments," in Dean Baker, Gerald Epstein, and Robert Pollin, eds., *Globalization and Progressive Economic Policy* (New York: Cambridge University Press, 1998), p. 64.

3. Michael J. Mandel, "The High-Risk Society; New Key to Economic Survival: Coping with Uncertainty," *Business Week*, October 28, 1996.

4. Ibid.

5. "The End of the Company Pension: Passing the Buck," *The Economist*, May 15, 1999.

6. "Surplus Problems," *The Economist*, August 15, 1998; also see Warren Hoge, "Swedish Party Pledging Expanded Welfare Gains Slim Victory," *New York Times*, September 21, 1998.

CHAPTER 4

1. Jeffrey Sachs, op. cit.

2. Nikolai Bukharin, *Imperialism and World Economy* (New York: Monthly Review Press), p. 26.

3. Ibid., p. 36.

4. Martin J. Sklar, *The Corporate Restructuring of American Capitalism, 1890–1916: The Market, the Law, and the Politics* (New York: Cambridge University Press, 1988), p. 81.

5. James Crotty, Gerald Epstein, and Patricia Kelly, "Multinational Corporations in the Neo-Liberal Regime," in Baker, Epstein, and Pollin op. cit., p. 121.

6. Martin Wolf, "Unreal Remedy," *Financial Times*, March 10, 1999.

7. Ibid.

8. Nicholas D. Kristof with David E. Sanger, "How U.S. Wooed Asia to Let Cash Flow In," *New York Times*, February 16, 1999.

9. Ibid.

10. David Felix, "On Financial Blowups and Authoritarian Regimes," in Jonathan Hartlyn and Samuel A. Morley, eds., *Latin American Political Economy: Financial Crisis and Political Change* (Boulder: Westview Press), pp. 95–6.

11. Ute Pieper and Lance Taylor, "The Revival of the Liberal Creed: The IMF, the World Bank and Inequality in a Globalized Economy," in Baker, Epstein, and Pollin, op. cit., p. 37.

12. J. M. Blaut, *The Colonizer's Model of the World: Geographical Diffusion and Euro-centric History* (New York: Guilford Press, 1995), p. 25.

13. Michael T. Klare, "The Clinton Doctrine," *The Nation*, April 19, 1999.

14. "Future of a Delusion," *The Progressive*, June 1999.

15. "New Visions for NATO," *New York Times*, December 7, 1998.

16. Benjamin Schwarz and Christopher Layne, "The Case Against Intervention in Kosovo," *The Nation*, April 19, 1999, p. 15.

17. William Hartung, "NATO Boondoggle," *The Progressive*, May 1998.

18. See Lora Lumpe and Jeff Donarski, *The Arms Trade Revealed: A Guide for Investigators and Activists* (Federation of American Scientists, n.d.); Anna Rich, "U.S. Exports Arms to the World," *Resist*, May 1999.

19. Ellen Meiksins Wood, "Kosovo and the New Imperialism," *Monthly Review,* June 1999, p. 3.

CHAPTER 5

1. See the 1999 UN *Human Development Report.*

2. Philip S. Golub, "When East Asia Falters," *Le Monde Diplomatique*, July 1998.

3. Ibid.

4. On the Japanese postwar system and the ways it combined a basically corrupt financial sector with an effective bureaucratic-led industrialization, see William K. Tabb, *The Postwar Japanese System: Cultural Economy and Economic Transformation* (New York: Oxford University Press, 1995), and on growth theory more broadly, William K. Tabb, *Reconstructing Political Economy: The Great Divide in Economic Thought* (London and New York: Routledge, 1999), chapter 10.

5. James Fallows, "How the Far East Was Won," *U.S. News & World Report*, December 8, 1997.

6. Steven Pearlstein and Tim Smart, "Confronting a Deepening Asian Crisis," *Washington Post National Weekly Edition*, December 1997.

7. *Business Week*, October 13, 1997.

8. *The Economist*, November 15, 1997.

9. Henry Kissinger, "The United States and Europe: What Are We Trying to Do?" *Trilateral Commission 1998 Berlin Meetings Proceedings*, p. 47.

10. Martin Feldstein, "Refocusing the IMF," *Foreign Affairs* 77:2 (March/April 1998), p. 27.

11. Robert Wade, "The Asian Debt-and-Development Crisis of 1997–9: Causes and Consequences," *World Development, August 1999.*

12. Jagdish Bhagwati, "The Capital Myth," *Foreign Affairs* 77:3 (May/June 1998).

13. John Eatwell, "International Capital Liberalization: The Record," Working Paper, Center for Economic Policy Analysis at the New School for Social Research, New York.

14. Martin Wolf, Comments to *Trilateral Commission 1998 Berlin Meetings Proceedings*, p.11 (emphasis added).

15. Kiichi Miyazawa, "Understanding and Addressing the Asian Financial Crisis," *Trilateral Commission 1998 Berlin Meetings Proceedings*.

16. Jeffrey Sachs, "The IMF and the Asian Flu," op. cit.

17. Jerome I. Levinson, "The International Financial System: A Flawed Architecture," *Fletcher Forum of World Affairs Journal*, Winter/Spring 1999, pp. 38–9.

CHAPTER 6

1. Eric Schmitt, "How a Fierce Backlash Saved the 'Made in America' Label," *New York Times*, December 6, 1997.

2. "It's a complicated issue and we tried," said Jodie Z. Bernstein of the Federal Trade Commission's Bureau of Consumer Protection and a thirty-year veteran of the regulatory wars, "but we just didn't communicate the proposal well enough." Ibid.

3. Thomas L. Friedman, "Don't Punish Africa," *New York Times*, March 7, 2000.

4. L. J. Davis, "A Deadly Dearth of Drugs," *Mother Jones*, January/February 2000.

5. "Malaria 'Has Cost Africa $100bn GDP,' " *Financial Times*, April 25, 2000.

6. Carlos Vilas, "The Decline of the Steady Job in Latin America," *NACLA Report on the Americas*, Jan./Feb. 1999.

CHAPTER 7

1. William R. Cline, *Trade and Income Distribution* (Washington, D.C.: Institute for International Economics, 1997).

2. Reed Abelson, "Part-Time Work for Some Adds Up to Full-Time Job," *New York Times*, November 2, 1998.

3. Mary Williams Walsh, "As Overtime Rises, Fatigue Becomes Labor Issue," *New York Times*, September 17, 2000.

4. Peter Coy, "Help! I'm a Prisoner in a Shrinking Cubicle," *Business Week*, August 4, 1997.

5. Diane Brady, "Why Service Stinks," *Business Week*, October 23, 2000.

6. Paul C. Judge, "What've You Done for Us Lately?" *Business Week*, September 14, 1998.

7. Diane Brady, "Why Service Stinks," p. 126.

8. Ursula Hews, "The Making of a Cybertariat: Virtual Work in the Real World," in Leo Panitch and Colin Leys, eds., *Socialist Register 2001: Working Classes, Global Realities* (London: Merlin Press, 2000), p. 16.

9. "The Surveillance Society," *The Economist*, May 1, 1999, in a special May Day feature on "The End of Privacy."

10. Edward Luttwak, *Turbo Capitalism: Winners and Losers in the Global Economy* (New York: HarperCollins, 2000).

11. "Welch's March to the South," *Business Week*, December 6, 1999.

12. Michelle Conlin, "Hey, What About Us?" *Business Week*, December 27, 1999.

13. John Gerard Ruggie, *Constructing the World Polity: Essays on International Institutionalization* (London: Routledge, 1998), p. 196.

14. Kate Bronfenbrenner, *Uneasy Terrain: The Impact of Capital Mobility on Workers, Wages and Union Organizing* (Washington: U.S. Trade Deficit Review Commission, 1999). <www.ustdrc.gov>

15. Program on International Policy Attitudes 2000, as reported in "Seattle Comes to Washington," *The Economist*, April 15, 2000.

16. United Nations Conference on Trade and Development, *World Investment Report 1997: Transnational Corporations, Market Structure and Competition Policy* (New York: UN, 1997).

17. Michael Zweig, *The Working-Class Majority* (Ithaca: Cornell University/ILR Press, forthcoming).

18. Amy Borrus and Richard S. Dinham, with Lorraine Woellert, Catherine Yang, and Jim Kestetter, "Tech: The Virtual Third Party," *Business Week*, April 24, 2000, p. 84.

19. Thomas L. Friedman, "Corporations on Steroids," *New York Times*, February 4, 2000.

20. Mike France, "The Unseemly Campaign of Mr. Microsoft," *Business Week*, April 24, 2000.

CHAPTER 8

1. Steven Greenhouse, "Nike's Chief Cancels a Gift over Monitor of Sweatshops," *New York Times*, April 25, 2000.

2. Elaine Bernard, "The WTO in Seattle: What It Was All About," *Washington Post National Weekly Edition*, December 13, 1999.

3. "Reader's Report," *Business Weekly*, May 22, 2000.

4. Richard Rorty, "Looking Backward from the Year 2096," in *Philosophy and Social Hope* (New York: Penguin Putnam, 1999), p. 243.

5. Richard Rorty, ""Back to Class Politics," in *Philosophy and Social Hope* (New York: Penguin Putnam, 1999), p. 257.

Index